D1601574

12 Truths to Change Your Marriage

A Respect Dare Journey

By Nina Roesner

12 Truths To Change Your Marriage

© 2014 Nina Roesner. All rights reserved. No portion of this book may be reproduced, stored in a retrieval system, or transmitted in any form or by any means – electronic, mechanical, photocopy, recording, or any other – except for brief quotations in printed reviews, without the prior permission of the publisher.

Published by Greater Impact, 554 Belle Meade Farm Drive, Loveland, OH 45140

Scriptures are taken from the following: The Holy Bible, New International Version. Copyright © 1973, 1978, 1984, International Bible Society. Used by permission of Zondervan Bible Publishers. The Holy Bible, New Living Translation®. Copyright © 1996. Used by permission of Tyndale House Publishers, Inc., Wheaton, Illinois 60189. All rights reserved. The New American Standard Bible®. Copyright © 1960, 1962, 1963, 1968, 1971, 1972,1973,1975, 1995 by The Lockman Foundation. Used by permission. The King James Version of the Bible. Public domain. The New King James Version®. Copyright © 1982 by Thomas Nelson, Inc. Used by permission. All rights reserved. The Message by Eugene H. Peterson. Copyright © 1993, 1994, 1995, 1996, 2000, 2001, 2002. Used by permission of NavPress Publishing Group. All rights reserved.

Disclaimer: The names and details surrounding many of the stories have been changed to protect the identity of individuals. Any association with specific individuals is purely unintended.

Printed in the United States of America.

12 Truths to Change Your Marriage

by Nina Roesner

FOR WIVES . . .

IN HONOR OF THE *DAUGHTERS OF SARAH*, WHO ACTIVELY LIVE OUT EPHESIANS 5:33:

AND THE WIFE MUST RESPECT HER HUSBAND.

YOU ARE HER DAUGHTERS IF YOU DO WHAT IS RIGHT AND DO NOT GIVE WAY TO FEAR. ... SPEAKING THE TRUTH IN LOVE, WE WILL GROW TO BECOME IN EVERY RESPECT THE MATURE BODY OF HIM WHO IS THE HEAD, THAT IS, CHRIST.

1 PETER 3:6; EPHESIANS 4:15

Table of Contents: ~

INTRODUCTION

We are humbled at the work God is doing, and privileged to be a small part of it. This book has been a labor of love, a project that took nearly three years to complete from concept to finished copy. Being a writer is an odd experience for me. Even after authoring a couple of books and blogging for several years, I still don't consider myself an author. I'm a professional trainer. I am humbled by your trust in the small part I'm playing in the story He's writing in your life.

The first thing you need to understand is that this is a book steeped in Biblical truth and real life experiences. I hesitate to call it "religious," but I will tell you that our goal is to provide you with the foundation for better understanding God, your husband, and yourself—enough to impact all your relationships. I am not a degreed theologian and I am 100 percent certain there are many others wiser than I. However, the contents of this book are a reflection of years of study combined with the experiences we have witnessed in *Daughters of Sarah*®, *The Respect Dare*® E-Course, and *The Respect Dare* Small Group Study. Of course, my own marriage and personal relationships have played a part in the creation of this book as well.

The Bible provides many contrasts between wise (mature) and unwise (immature) behavior and, when Biblical wisdom is applied to our relationships—how we view ourselves, God, and others—we begin to see the change we desperately long for in our lives. As we mature (become wise) as Christians, we find the peace, joy, and comfort promised to us by following Jesus. When we refuse to mature, we choose a harder path.

This book is different from *The Respect Dare,* which Thomas Nelson Publishers released in December 2012. The first *Respect Dare* is an experiential devotional containing examples of respect, interaction with God's Word, introspective questions, along with a series of dares to complete.

12 Truths to Change Your Marriage is designed to provide you with foundational knowledge from the Bible, professional research, and the experiences of the many women who have taken either our training course for wives associated with *The Respect Dare* or our *Daughters of Sarah®* course.

12 Truths To Change Your Marriage will provide more information about a wife's experience of marriage, while still offering some introspection and some practical dares based on research and Biblical truth. *The Respect Dare* has a small group guide available. With *12 Truths*, it is easy to lead a discussion group by sharing what you write as you work your way through each chapter. We are also using it as the companion book to our *Daughters of Sarah®* Training Course.

While this book is less experiential than *The Respect Dare,* we hope to offer, in a different format, many of the same truths. It makes no difference which book you read and experience first.

We do not pretend to offer "the last word" on marriage. Nor do we attempt to add to or replace the Bible. Rather, we hope to be a part of your journey and are privileged to be joining you on the path. The journey to a better marriage takes years and is not for the faint of heart; however, it is the context through which we become women of strength and dignity in all our relationships. Everyone on our team at Greater Impact is still working on these things. We are excited to share what we have learned on our journey.

Truth #1:
What You Really Believe About God and The Bible Impacts Your Relationships.

Before launching into this material too deeply, I want to share the basic theology to which I subscribe and a process we have witnessed that often occurs in marriages. This process may be familiar to you to some degree already. It also is an approach with which we have seen many women struggle through. Fortunately, there is a ton of research about all these things. Dr. John Gottman has been studying what causes divorce for many years and his research is well-known in the field of psychology. We will talk about his research, but understand that the practice that we have seen unfold in our ministry lines up with what is supported by this research, and what is already in the Bible. The very good news here is that we can give you an outline of the approach and you can evaluate where you are within it. As a result of reading this book, you will most likely be able to have a positive impact on your marriage and grow closer to God. We are excited to be able to present you with tangible help, along with the encouragement to align your heart with godly motives.

If you have many issues with defensiveness and criticism in your marriage and few positive interactions, there is much you can personally do to impact things. Gottman demonstrated in his research that healthy and happy relationships have a ratio of twenty positive interactions to each negative one on average. During conflict, there are five positive interactions compared to each negative. Happy couples are *gentle* with each other. Unhappy relationships exhibit .8 positive interactions for every negative. The good news is that the Bible has a ton of wise and helpful practical information about how to create healthy relationships. We also highly recommend Dr. Gottman's materials if your husband is interested in growing with you as a spouse.

Another positive is that most of the time one person's positive influence can create an environment that naturally encourages positive behavior from another. These marriages are typical of what we hear from the many women who read and do the dares in The Respect Dare (Thomas Nelson, 2012) and/or participate in Daughters of Sarah. Unfortunately, the not-so-good news is that there some people who cannot receive love or affection easily. They may be deeply defensive, mentally ill, or so spiritually or emotionally immature that they will need to be confronted, potentially with others, to impact any kind of positive health in the relationship. If you are the person who has been confronted and are on the receiving end of an ultimatum from your husband, know that the absolute best news is that God is in the redemption business and He can help you turn your situation completely around if you will choose to follow Him. You might be unfamiliar with what that even means, and this book will help you grow in that area, especially if you are trying to create health and positivity in your marriage.

I realize there are many facets of Christianity and you will have to be discerning about how what we suggest applies to your situation. There are probably many elements of theology that are irrelevant to a discussion on marriage—like the age of the earth, for example. Here I will discuss only what is relevant. First, I believe in the Holy Trinity—God as simultaneously three beings within Himself: the Father, the Son as Jesus Christ, and the Holy Spirit.

We also use the word, "Christian" to describe someone who believes that Jesus is Lord of his or her life, that Christ was both God and God's son, and that He was crucified and rose to life again as a payment for our individual sins, and confesses this truth aloud to others (Romans 10:9-10). Words can have different connotations. For example, the word, "Christian," has a positive connotation to most of those who follow Christ. For those who are atheists, satanists, or even some Christians who have been wounded by the church, the word has a negative connotation, even to the point of stirring up hate. I don't like labels; but for convenience, I will use some throughout the book.

I do not fit perfectly into any specific category or denomination of Christianity. My husband, Jim, and I are members of an Evangelical Free Church of America (denominational) church. I also visit other churches in our area when doing classes, and can worship easily at any of them. At the time of this writing, there are essentially two "camps" of belief categories about marriage: Egalitarian and Complementarian. Humans like to label things to be able to talk about them, but one of the problems with labels is they don't fully capture the entire idea. Then, after the label has been around for a while, so much discussion has occurred that the original meanings get distorted and facets of them become extreme. This has happened with the terms egalitarian and complementarian.

I appreciate elements of egalitarianism, particularly the emphasis on the equal value with which men and women should be viewed. When talking about marriage, many egalitarians strongly emphasize the friendship element as talked about in Titus 2. This *phileo* love that a wife is to have for her husband is the "friendship" kind of love that is extremely important to a man. Christians for Biblical Equality define what they believe as quoted from their website:

- We believe in the equality and essential dignity of men and women of all ethnicities, ages, and classes. We recognize that all persons are made in the image of God and are to reflect that image in the community of believers, in the home, and in society.
- We believe that men and women are to diligently develop and use their God-given gifts for the good of the home, church and society.[1]

I don't disagree with anything written above. Enough debate has occurred over time, however, that some extreme complementarians would take issue with my being supportive of the above core beliefs. I have spoken

---

[1] Christians for Biblical Equality
https://www.Wikipedia.org/wiki/Christian_Egalitarianism#cite_note-12

to groups and talked about being your husband's friend, and have had some in the extreme complementarian camp get upset with me.

The complementarians define themselves essentially as having equal but complementary roles in marriage. Men are tasked with providing, leading, and protecting. Women are tasked with nurturing, caring, and submitting to their husband's leadership.

Like the complementarians, I also subscribe to the Biblical concepts of submission, respect, and the husband's responsibility for the family. I have said this and been verbally attacked by egalitarians, however, which I find interesting, because the nature of the verses really is not any different than the nature of the ones they teach. None of these are rooted in the gospels and the words of Christ, but rather the other books in the New Testament. A few years ago, I did a ton of research on the verses in Ephesians which talk about a husband being the "head of his wife" as Christ is the "head of the church." As is the case with literally everything on the internet, information seemed conflicting. Some writers even went so far as to blatantly lie about whether or not the word, "head" ever referred to any type of leadership position in the Bible. There were even writers that said it did not, in support of egalitarian thought, but that is simply not true. What is true is that deep research into those verses shows us that the word *head* often means "in charge of" in the original texts. The word also meant a literal "head" and is used in the Bible and the culture in regard to decapitation and with regard to leaders of tribes.

Some scholars say that when the Bible was written, our hearts ruled us, not our mind or "head." Some like to define the word "head" as "source," because the head is the source of life. However, Christ Himself is really the source because our husbands are human. The verse also is tied to a reference to Christ and the church, which does not specifically portray leadership, but rather sacrifice and servant-hood. When looking at the original language, I prefer to think of "head" in this verse as "brings life" both because without it there is death and also that is what Christ came to do — bring abundant life to His church. I also see it as "accountable one," somewhat like a CEO is accountable for the actions of his company, or a governor is accountable for his state. The United States had a rather harsh winter in 2014 and news reports of people being stuck in traffic for over ten hours made headlines in Atlanta. The governor of Georgia held a press conference in which he took accountability for the lack of salt trucks and preparation his state was able to make for its citizens. In reality, he had someone who was elected or hired to deal with these sorts of things, but it wasn't them you saw taking the heat – it was the governor. This concept also applies to our husbands – God holds them accountable.

So in looking at *head* in the original language, another phrase that appears indicates a "source of life" in reference to "head." While we would not use this etymology to make a specific definition, we could then infer that our husbands could bring us life as Christ brings life to the church and that they are accountable for the outcome of the family. Even with that nuance of understanding, those phrases are still a mystery, as specifically stated in Ephesians 5. In other words, we probably will not fully understand them.

In researching the use of "submission" and the topic of women's roles in marriage, some complementarian writers even go so far as to support following a husband into sinful behavior and accepting abuse. None of that is legitimate, either. Given that both egalitarian and complementarian extremists exist, it is my humble opinion one cannot put a lot of faith in the definitions of the labels any longer.

Regarding hierarchy and responsibility, we view the husband as "head" of his home, but not the only person God speaks to. Rather, he is the one He holds accountable first. We do not believe the husband is equal to Christ. He is a sinner; Christ is not.

We appreciate the elements of complementarianism that say a man needs a wife's help and that the genders complete each other. Again, neither is "better" or "less than" but simply different with different strengths.

There are extreme facets of complementarianism that we believe are inaccurate and even dangerous. Some support the belief that women should submit in all things, to such an extreme as to not even confront their husbands' sin against them. Respectfully, we disagree. If God leads, women should confront their husbands, with love in a gentle way, respectfully – in the same way as one would hope a Christian husband, with Christ as his model, also would try to lead. Gentle, loving communication in an atmosphere absent of defensiveness, contempt, disdain or argumentativeness brings Christ's example to leadership and submission within marriage.

We also disagree that women should not lead worship or write or lead mix-gendered groups in church situations. I do not feel called to preach to a church therefore I'm staying out of the debate about women pastors. You may feel called to pursue this; I do not. I have enough on my plate with the marriage topic and raising my kids so I am asking that we abstain from dialogue on this. The research and study I have done is in regard to marriage. That being said, I am asking for grace from you on my lack of involvement and research with the issue of women in the pulpit. I do appreciate the male leadership in my church. They also appreciate me, and we have a mutually respectful relationship. I know enough about gender differences in brain physiology to know there will probably always be men who simply cannot learn from a woman. The converse of that also is true.

Because of the way our brains are wired, women typically have the ability to transfer experiences—to learn something in one situation and use that knowledge in a completely different situation. Brain wiring makes this more difficult for men. Because they generally lack the ability to transfer, they often have difficulty learning from women instructors due to the examples women typically use, which are often unrelated to a man's world. However, I also have known talented women teachers who employ sports or business examples that help men make those connections. Like the average woman, I typically utilize relationship examples in my teaching. However, when I teach mixed-gender classes, both professionally and within the church, I make sure to incorporate business examples and ensure that my teaching staff includes men, due to the fact that I am aware that, in general, men and women receive information differently.

Having said all of this, however, I still believe there is a hierarchy in marriage and a partnering which occurs in the most mature of relationships. This is based on the verses in Genesis 2 and 3. These verses tell about Eve being created from Adam's rib and God holding Adam responsible first for what happened to speak to Adam's position as "head." Adam also specifically names Eve as the "woman you gave me," (blaming God and Eve, but that is another discussion), which indicates she was a gift for Adam and not the other way around. Wives also are told to submit to our husbands in Colossians 3:18 and Ephesians 5:22. Because we are told to become one flesh, however, there is a unity, a corporate-ness that we need to perceive in this unit.

And what about the concept of mutual submission? Ephesians 5:21 says, "Submit to one another out of reverence for Christ." Again, it's a willingness to "place yourself under someone else" or to "subordinate our rights to someone else's," which exists beautifully when both husband and wife are growing in maturity in their relationship with God. Because women are more relationship oriented than men[2], we also will often subordinate our rights earlier. In a marriage, it is fairly common for people to mature at different rates. As men and women become more mature Christians, they have a

---

[2] http://www.columbiaconsult.com/pubs/v52_fall07.html

gentler, more respectful, more loving and affectionate attitude toward each other. Based on what we have seen in thousands of marriages around the country and based on what we have researched, selfishness runs rampant in immature relationships, while selflessness is the hallmark of mature relationship.

The best thing we can ever hope or pray for our husband (or anyone else, for that matter!) is that he will fall madly in love with Christ Jesus and make Him Lord of his life, choosing to follow Him. As we pursue a relationship with Christ, we become filled with the Holy Spirit and we literally become God's love to the world, beginning with our own relationships at home.

As parents, we naturally literally subjugate ourselves to our babies needs in order to raise them and to take care of them: when newborns, we check on every cry and sacrifice sleep, showers, and often elements of our careers and professional status as we choose to pour into them with little return. At our house, we do not watch much television, and when we do, we choose things in which our youngest child can participate. We do not resent our children when we sacrifice, but we do tend to resent the person we are married to if he is not behaving as selflessly as we think we are because we do not naturally see him as a spiritual being on his own journey in need of grace. We see him as we would view ourselves – in other words, we judge. Most of us, however, can see children as less mature and more in need of grace. Therefore, we more easily extend grace to them, often not taking their behaviors personally. Adults, however, are viewed through our own lens of equality (adulthood), and we expect them to behave as we think we would in a given situation.

We also will do what is good for our children more readily than another adult, particularly our husbands. We will hold on to driving privileges or give constructive coaching in an effort to help our children. We will let little Jessie know when what she said is mean or hurtful, but often withhold this information from adults who hurt us. With our husband, we tend to swing to extremes either nagging or doing things for him as if he were a young child, or avoid addressing his hurtful or neglectful behavior altogether. Neither approach is healthy. It is not "good" for our husbands to engage in destructive, abusive, or sinful behaviors, but often we fail to address his behavior kindly, in an effort to be "submissive." There is little teaching on this topic in our culture; however, we will attempt to shed some light on it.

An example of this playing out might be the simple hope that we have of a birthday card or gift. We would not be disappointed if our small child did not know it was our birthday and because of that lack of knowledge did not buy us a gift, make or get a card for us, or even say, "Happy Birthday." If our husband, sister, or friends forget, we are likely to be disappointed because we see adults differently. We judge more easily. When we are more mature, however, we can more easily forgive, extend grace, and not take things personally. We do not establish our value as based on another person's behavior or lack thereof and, as a result, we do not judge, we are not easily disappointed, and we connect our value to God's opinion of us instead. A mature response might be, "Hey, today's my birthday; let's go do something to celebrate it."

Having said all that, know that when both marriage partners are mature and can view each other as brother and sister in Christ, they can more easily serve each other with the love of Christ. Trouble occurs when we view our needs as more important than our husbands', or our kids', etc. We are called to love, to serve, to live as Christ. Women are told specifically to subject themselves to their husbands (as he is seen by God as responsible for the family) and everyone is told to do that with all believers. *It has nothing, whatsoever, to do with equality.*

And with no caveat as to where our husband is in his journey, the Bible commands us to submit to him. This willing subordination best displays itself in marriage when you and your husband are making decisions and cannot agree. We are told in Ephesians 5:22 to submit to our husbands "in all things." This does not, however, put him in a position of having to direct, organize, and manage everything, as if we are his puppets or even his personal assistant, nor are wives ever equated with slaves anywhere in the Bible. If he is a wise leader, he will avoid being controlling and not try to micro-manage his wife or children. When he and his wife have different opinions, it means things are talked about. If he is a wise leader, he will consider her input, as she sees many things he does not. If we cannot get to a place where we share the same decision, we should willingly choose to do what he suggests. In other words, we are actively choosing to not be disagreeable in the way we disagree, and respectful in the way we accept that he is held accountable for the beginl:

family. If he is an unwise or immature leader, it will be more challenging but still necessary for his wife to submit and respect him. We will also address this issue.

Your attitude toward his leadership matters greatly in your relationship with your husband. I will explain this in more detail later, but for now know that human brain chemistry has you, as a woman, wired for this necessity of submission in marriage and he also is wired to need you to receive his leadership. Whether we like it or not, hierarchy exists in all organizations: wolf pack, country, or corporation. Someone is responsible. In a marriage, God holds the husband as that person. Hierarchy also seems to exist in the Trinity, with Jesus Christ Himself submitting to the Father's will after begging Him: "Take this cup from me, but not my will, but Thine be done," the night before His crucifixion. Given that all Three are God, obviously this is a difficult concept to wrap our brains around.

I believe in the Trinity as described in the Bible. I believe Jesus Christ is both God and the Son of God. I believe He died for our sins, paying the penalty for those sins; and that He conquered death and rose from the grave on the third day. I believe He actively chose to submit to His Father's authority, even though He clearly did not want to go through the suffering ahead of Him.

If we choose to follow Christ, we need to understand submission because we need to submit to God. I believe I am a sinner and will always be a sinner. However, I am also a saint saved by believing in Jesus Christ, confessing Him with my mouth and making Him Lord of my life as explained in Romans 10:9: *"Because, if you confess with your mouth that Jesus is Lord and believe in your heart that God raised him from the dead, you will be saved."* I believe the most amazing thing about Jesus is that we can have a relationship with Him. He is a real person and He is God. Without submission, however, our relationship with God is severely lacking. *Much of our ability to hear from God is rooted in the level to which we obey Him.*

God's own Word tells us this in John 14 (emphasis mine):

> *6 Jesus answered, "I am the way and the truth and the life. **No one** comes to the Father except through me. 7 If you really knew me, you would know my Father as well. From now on, you do know him and have seen him." 8 Philip said, "Lord, show us the Father and that will be enough for us." 9 Jesus answered: "Don't you know me, Philip, even after I have been among you such a long time? **Anyone who has seen me has seen the Father**. How can you say, 'Show us the Father'? 10 Don't you believe that I am in the Father, and that the Father is in me? The words I say to you are not just my own. Rather, it is the Father, living in me, who is doing his work. 11 **Believe me when I say that I am in the Father and the Father is in me**; or at least believe on the evidence of the miracles themselves.*

> *12 I tell you the truth, anyone who has faith in me will do what I have been doing. He will do even greater things than these, because I am going to the Father. 13 And I will do whatever you ask in my name, so that the Son may bring glory to the Father. 14 You may ask me for anything in my name, and I will do it. 15 "**If you love me, you will***

obey what I command. 16 And I will ask the Father, and he will give you another Counselor to be with you forever - 17 the Spirit of truth. The world cannot accept him, because it neither sees him nor knows him. **But you know him, for he lives with you and will be in you.** *18 I will not leave you as orphans; I will come to you. 19 Before long, the world will not see me anymore, but you will see me. Because I live, you also will live. 20 On that day you will realize that I am in my Father, and you are in me, and I am in you.*

21 **Whoever has my commands and obeys them, he is the one who loves me.** *He who loves me will be loved by my Father, and I too will love him and show myself to him." 22 Then Judas (not Judas Iscariot) said, "But, Lord, why do you intend to show yourself to us and not to the world?" 23 Jesus replied,* **"If anyone loves me, he will obey my teaching. My Father will love him, and we will come to him and make our home with him. 24 He who does not love me will not obey my teaching.** *These words you hear are not my own; they belong to the Father who sent me.*

I believe the Bible is Truth – and I believe the entire Bible is true, and therefore, we need to look at the entire Bible when we discuss what it has to say about any particular topic, including marriage. We need to look at it with the understanding that we are to submit to God's word, the Bible, *and in doing so, we open a door in our very soul for God to dwell (make His home, verse 23) inside of us, enabling us to hear from God Himself.* Our obedience is directly tied to the level with which we hear from God.

At Greater Impact, we so strongly believe these things that we are coining a phrase: wholetarian.

wholetarian
noun \ˈhōl-ə-ˈter-ē-ən\
: complete or full: not lacking or leaving out any part of Biblical truth as it applies to marriage
: having all of the Bible verses about marriage

This word is used currently in reference to the "whole foods" movement, but I believe the second definition above also is in order. We are very simply just trying to state that the entire Bible is true.

I believe that once you start "picking and choosing" what applies or discounting any of the Bible, you have to discount it all. I do not, however, believe only one translation is inspired. I've seen God use many different translations to speak to His children. I do not believe the Bible is simply an "overall good idea," but rather a living document that can (and does) speak into the daily moments of our lives. I believe looking into the original language provides additional understanding, but I also believe that if you didn't have access to the original language, the words alone would speak into your life at the time you needed them, regardless of what translation you had access to.

The Bible teaches that women are equal to men. Neither gender is better or less than the other. There are differences between the genders, differences between people, and, therefore, differences between marriages. You will hear me speak, however, in generalities. Research indicates some specific trends in behavior, psychology, and in physiology[3]. I mean no offense when I do not address those outside the trends. Even my own marriage does not always fit into the "average" category in a few areas. Generalities help us develop our foundation of understanding and are worth exploring. They also will apply to most of the people most of the time.

We encourage ongoing communication between you and your husband. Communication is paramount to the success of a marriage. Miscommunication or lack of communication often sows seeds of discontent and discouragement based on lies and is responsible for the destruction of many marriages.

I believe that marriages look different because there are different people involved. I have a friend who would adopt more than the nine kids she already has . . . and probably will. Jim and I are not called to that. This does not mean that we are wrong or not as good as parents compared to my friend and her husband either.

I have studied for more than twenty years and I am comfortable in the Truth God has revealed to me. He has confirmed these things, told me to share them, and given me a message. I claim Christ as King and ruler of my life. I am His bondservant, His slave. He does not work for me, but rather, the other way around. I exist to delight Him.

---

[3] Shaunti Feldhahn, The Male Factor, Broadway Books, 2009

My life is for His use, for His glory, for however He sees fit: nothing else.

For a long time I have sensed God calling an army of women to wrap their arms, brains, and hearts around the concept of applied respect and to create a family environment where His light shines as never before. I believe that time is *now*. I am honored you are considering joining us. I know I am asking you to do something hard. I am asking you, first and foremost, to draw nearer to God by obeying Him. You will find your relationship with Him dramatically improves as a result.

I also am warning you that you will suffer because you have chosen to grow. Unfortunately, pain is the Biblical route to growth. I wish it were not, but it is. Also, know He means the suffering for good; although often it won't seem like it at the time. Like *The Respect Dare,* this book is a speedy trip on the road to killing selfishness—and, because of that, it will be difficult.

Submission can be difficult. Respect also can be difficult. Submission and respect are often just as difficult (or even harder, in some cases) as confronting your husband's sin, especially when it is something we humans judge as heinous. I'm glad you are here. It's a road paved with tears, a journey tough on the soles of your feet, as well as your heart. But He is in the transformation business, making all things new—and always He begins with our hearts.

Let's get started.

Truth #2:

God is Someone with Whom You can have a Real Relationship

I sat in the bleachers surrounded by hundreds of other teenagers at the University of Wisconsin listening to the keynote speaker. Over the course of the week of camp (I was a baton-twirling majorette), I had grown to admire and eagerly soak up all the words this man shared. It was the last session of the camp and his final words floored me and caused me to rethink everything I thought I knew about him. He said, "If you can believe, you CAN achieve! But none of that achievement matters – the secret to happiness truly comes from serving other people and following Christ." He lost me at "serving other people" because that did not fit into my philosophy. "Serving Christ" then labeled him as one of "those" people. I was not quite sure who "those" people were, but I knew I did not want to give up my pursuit of success to serve others.

As someone who did not grow up in any faith tradition and was an atheist from my teens until I became engaged, I really do understand confusion or distrust toward religion.

I have been there. I have fully doubted the existence of God, and His goodness. I have viewed organized religion as frivolous and an activity for those with such weakness mentally that they succumb to believing in fairy tales.

Maybe you have been there, too – or maybe you are there now. Can I gently ask that you just hear me out? Make your way through the book and at the end, hopefully at a minimum, you will understand what some of us who follow Christ believe. I know this is a confusing journey you are on – and you just want to improve your marriage. There are many out there saying that to follow God you have to "do" all these things. However, the truth is we simply have to receive His gift and then set about the business of getting to know Him. If there was one thing I could have you hear about religion it is this – forget it. Instead, I have this really good Friend I'd like you to meet. He's super smart, smarter than anyone you could even imagine, and He loves His friends really well – oh, and He wants to help you with your marriage, your parenting, and even has some really cool things you could get involved in with His family. He's always around and if you'd like to get to know Him, just say the word. After you get to know Him, you're going to want to spend more and more time with Him, and guess what? It's super easy to do that because He's always around. And He has a book of stories that gives His history so you can understand more about Him. His name is Jesus.

Christ is really the answer to the questions and problems you are facing in your marriage. The research out there also is pretty convincing as people of faith get divorced nearly 20 percent less than those who do not affiliate themselves with any religion.[4] That fact alone should make you wonder what Christians are doing that others are not. Those of us who know Him personally fall into that "religion" category, but what is really amazing is that we view our marriage radically differently than most people – and that's why we can stay married.

Recent big "A-Ha!" research findings from Shaunti Feldhahn's new book, *Highly Happy Marriages,*[5] is that couples that are actually happy are doing these things amongst others:

1. Paying attention to the "little signs of affection" daily – they matter a TON. We have a list of those for men and one for women on my blog at www.NinaRoesner.com to help you.
2. Believing the best about their spouse – happy couples frequently refer back to "I know she loves me" or "I know he doesn't mean that" instead of assuming the worst or creating a negative motive for their spouse.
3. Surprise – they go to bed mad. They don't do conflict late at night, often because they realize the outcome won't be good because they're tired.
4. They pay attention to the good things their spouse does – and thus do things their spouse likes, on purpose, to help them when they are having a rough spell. For example, "they pick up the slack" when the other is injured, stressed, or super-busy.
5. They choose to be in charge of their feelings instead of letting their feelings dictate their

---

[4] http://www.divorcestatistics.org
[5] Shaunti Feldhahn, The Surprising Secrets of Highly Happy Marriages, Multnomah Books, 2013, Veritas Enterprises.

behavior – which results in the ability to see what is True, Philippians 4:8 style.

6. They live in a state of conscious wonder – gratitude toward their spouse and what s/he does.

7. And the most important secret? They have Jesus Christ at the center of their marriage. Both husband and wife have deep relationship with Jesus Christ such that they serve each other happily and trust God with the outcome in tough situations.

That last point is one of the most important, in my opinion. Her book also contains a number of other helpful insights per her research. I included the above seven because they speak to what we are talking about in this book and in the Daughters of Sarah Experience.

Whose Life Is It Anyway?

I grew up around many people living out the philosophy "he who dies with the most toys wins." But even as a child, I knew I could not take what I accumulated here on earth with me when I died. Even so, I deeply sought achievement in everything. How much we focus on maintaining or creating the lifestyle we want indicates our priorities. This focus also is a reflection of our maturity in God's economy. Are we like a three-year-old tightly grasping his fire engine, proclaiming, "No! Mine!" when the opportunity to share arises? Or are we mature enough to give freely? Do we choose wisely with our time, focusing only on what God asks of us? In God's economy, relationships matter more than financial well-being. Having healthy relationships with God and others reflects our level of maturity and can bring great rewards. *Part of the reason the journey to a healthier place is filled with suffering and pain because our selfish nature dies as part of the process.* This death is painful.

Loving God and loving others are heralded as the most important things for us to do to follow Christ. Jesus Himself told a man that to have eternal life, the man needed to sell all that he had and follow Him.[6] Jesus was not suggesting that we all live communal lives and drop everything to become missionaries, but, rather, He knew that, for this man, his lifestyle was more important than love. Likewise, we have things we value more than our relationships, both with God and others. This creates disconnect between our values (as influenced by the culture) and our pursuit of holiness. It is my goal to help you uncover some common lies, reveal some Truth, and help you move forward in improving the most important relationships in your life:

- Your relationship with God
- Your relationship with yourself
- Your relationship with your husband
- Your relationship with your children and others

One morning, I had a revelation in Bible study as a young mom amidst women older and wiser than myself. We dialogued about that great commandment to love your God with all your heart, your soul, your mind and all your strength.[7] My throat tightened and tears welled as

---

[6] Luke 18:24-34
[7] Luke 10:27

sunlight streamed through the window onto the circle of women. The red flush of realization of my sin swept from my neck to my cheeks until I could contain the truth no longer. His teaching was gentle, but my reaction embarrassed me.

As my tears spilled, one of the older women asked me what was wrong and handed me a tissue. I dabbed at the mascara flecks on my cheeks, and confessed: *"I love my children more than I love God. I don't even* want *to love Him more than them."* I couldn't imagine the price I would pay for loving Him more—as if it would cost me something. Knowing looks and comforting nods and gentle murmurs of, "That's okay," and "Oh, that's perfectly natural, dear," and "Don't worry, about it," surrounded me.

Their hearts were loving and kind, but I also knew within my own heart that these feelings were wrong.

How harsh is that reality for you? For me, it was gut wrenching. I had reached a strange place in my journey. I realized that I was committing sin by not wanting to love God more than my kids. I thought of Abraham and his son, Isaac, whom he nearly sacrificed to God as the Lord tested his heart. I thought of Hannah turning over her son, Samuel, as young as a preschooler, to Eli the priest because she loved God enough to keep the vow she had made to Him. I couldn't imagine her sorrow. I thought of Mary and Jesus. For some reason, intense fear gripped my stomach.

I did not know it at the time, but this was my first hard battle with submission.

It was also my first battle with Love.

Our First Love

God wants to be first *in everything*. From Revelation 2 (emphasis mine):

> To the angel of the church in Ephesus write: The One who holds the seven stars in His right hand, the One who walks among the seven golden lampstands, says this: I know your deeds and your toil and perseverance, and that you cannot tolerate evil men, and you put to the test those who call themselves apostles, and they are not, and you found them to be false; and you have perseverance and have endured for My name's sake, and have not grown weary. *'But I have this against you, that you have left your first love. Therefore remember from where you have fallen, and repent and do the deeds you did at first; or else I am coming to you and will remove your lampstand out of its place—unless you repent.*

Knowing that God appreciates the work I do but has something against me should be terrifying. God destroyed cities with fire, cast plagues upon Egypt, and struck people dead for disobedience. I think of the New Testament demons that shudder when thinking about God (James 2:19), and I tremble at my lack of reverence. Have I bought the lie of the Christian culture, the one where we simply focus on how much He loves us? Have I subscribed to the thinking that because God is love, He no longer has His wrath? His Word to us is clear—return to putting Him first in our lives—and repent (be very sorry and change our behavior) or He will remove our lampstand out of its place. He is literally holding back judgment for the world. I do not pretend to understand fully for one single second what that last part of the verse actually means (neither do most scholars), but to think of being removed from something by Christ unless I repent cannot possibly be anything warm and fuzzy! It certainly cannot be anything the average person would consider "good."

Putting God first may mean a number of things to different people, but to me it seems simple. I know He is first in my life when
- I think of Him first thing in the morning, before I even get out of bed
- I spend time with Him first, before anyone else
- I praise Him first, before asking for anything
- I listen to His thoughts first, instead of starting with my laundry list of fears and needs
- I ask for His help in understanding His will first, before rattling off my agenda
- I listen to His Word and for His voice first, before deciding a course of action
- I ask Him to purpose my day for His purposes over my own
- I ask Him what He would do first, before considering my own opinion or the opinions of others
- I remember Him first when faced with His creation, decisions, celebrations, or troubles during the day

- I seek Him first with my family members and friends before—or instead of—offering up my advice and thoughts
- I remember Him first, thanking Him for the day, before closing my eyes and starting sleep

"First" assumes He is real and with me all day long. First acknowledges the realness of His person, and son, Jesus Christ. First equates with real relationship. And most important, I actually need to regularly ask His help in seeking Him first, because frankly, I frequently struggle with putting *myself* first instead.

He wants to be loved deeply with our all . . . first.

Unfortunately, we usually contact Him last, when we've exhausted all our resources on earth. Our ways are opposite or backward of His. The great commandment to love is found in the Old and New Testaments. Jesus was asked about the greatest commandment in the Law (Matthew 22:36–40). He responded by quoting the Old Testament, "'*Love the Lord your God with all your heart and with all your soul and with all your mind,*'" (which is found in Deuteronomy 6:5). Then He said (emphasis mine), "*This is the first and greatest commandment. And the second is like it: 'Love your neighbor as yourself.' All the Law and the Prophets hang on these two commandments.*"

The concept also is found in Leviticus 19:18. If we go back to that original verse, it says, quoting God Himself, "*Do not seek revenge or bear a grudge against anyone among your people, but love your neighbor as yourself. I am the Lord.*"

From the creation of time, the Word and voice of God births life into parched and dying relationships for those of His children who choose to receive His love and obey His commandments. How many times in your marriage have you been challenged by the temptation to seek revenge or bear a grudge against your husband? How different from God we are!

One year while on vacation for two weeks over the Christmas holiday, my husband and I had an abundance of negative interactions. Job stress and the pressure of each other's expectations yielded two exhausted grown-ups who acted less than their best. At one point I found myself harboring bitterness and resentment at some hurtful things my husband had done and said. Having attempted to talk through these things and the conversation ending in argument because of my own harsh start-up, I remember trying again. At one point I simply said through tears, "I know you didn't mean things the way I took them. I still need to just hear you say you are sorry. I need you to be sorry that I felt badly, because I need to forgive you, and I'm short in the grace department today. Sometimes I can do this without even talking to you or needing your apology, but this time I can't. I hurt and I just need you to say you are sorry about it."

He melted. I cried.

He apologized. I forgave.

We talked.

I understood he didn't mean things the way I heard them. I apologized for misreading his heart.

He forgave me.

We healed.

Is there a place for forgiveness in your marriage or in any of your relationships? I heard a pastor on a radio station say that if we don't get really good at forgiveness, we can expect all our relationships to be train wrecks. I believe that. I know I have found great healing for myself and my marriage and have facilitated forgiveness for both my husband and me by thinking through how I have wounded him and apologizing, or by gently confronting him when he has hurt me. Apology with communicated empathy and forgiveness are crucial to the foundational experience of love. We make mistakes and we sin. God gave us the tools of apology and forgiveness to keep our hearts free from the sins of bitterness and resentment, which are forms of selfish anger often based on lies. Sometimes God gives us enough grace to overlook others' sins against us and we can simply let the offenses go.

The blessing of love, the freedom of life abundant that comes from following Christ, is strangled by the sins of bitterness and resentment. These are born out of a lack of forgiveness. We need to process and forgive, asking God's help, otherwise our ability to give and receive love, both from God and others, will be stunted.

In 1 Corinthians 13 (ESV), the concept of love springs forth:

If I speak in the tongues of men and of angels, but have not love, I am a noisy gong or a clanging cymbal. And if I have prophetic powers, and understand all mysteries and all knowledge, and if I have all faith, so as to remove mountains, but have not love, I am nothing. If I give away all I have, and if I deliver up my body to be burned, but have not love, I gain nothing. Love is patient, and kind; love does not envy or boast; it is not arrogant or rude. It does not insist on its own way; it is not irritable or resentful; it does not rejoice at wrongdoing, but rejoices with the truth. Love bears all things; believes all things, hopes all things, endures all things.

The NIV also says in verse five, "*It does not dishonor others, it is not self-seeking, it is not easily angered, it keeps no record of wrongs.*"

For me, those verses slice my proud heart in two. I confess I have held grudges, been self-seeking, been impatient, unkind, proud, easily irritable and dishonorable toward God, my husband, and others. Frankly, I've been unbearable to live with sometimes instead of enduring all things! And I have not believed and hoped for the best, but instead expected the worst out of those I claim to love the most, including God and my husband and kids. If I am to be completely truthful, I am those things on any given day to a certain degree.

This lack of love for God is at the heart of much of our sin. I have realized and heard many more mature Christians say that as they have grown in their relationship with God, their love for Him and for others has increased. The deep desire to change, to become holy, is placed in us as He supernaturally transforms us into His likeness.[8] This is my experience as well—my sin nature is ever present, and I wish this was not so.

But the good news is that His love covers a multitude of sins and His mercies are new every morning. To the extent that we ourselves receive God's love and forgiveness, we will then extend it to others.

How about you?

1.   *To what degree have you received the gift of Jesus Christ? Have you done this "superficially?" Or at the "heart level?" How do you know?*

2.   *What do feel like God is asking you to do to deepen your relationship with Him?*

3.   *What will you do? When will you start?*

4.   *How much do you value the lifestyle you have, or the lifestyle you want, compared to your relationship with God? What do your thoughts and actions indicate is true for you right now?*

---

[8] 2 Corinthians 3:18 (ESV) And we all, with unveiled face, beholding the glory of the Lord, are being transformed into the same image from one degree of glory to another. For this comes from the Lord who is the Spirit.

5. *How freely do you extend grace to others? What does this reflect about how you've received God's grace yourself?*

6. *Where are you bearing a grudge or seeking revenge in your marriage? What do you do to your husband because of how he's treated you? Do you sense your actions are wrong?*

7. *What does your behavior and your heart say about who or what is first in your life?*

8. *What is the ONE thing you can start doing today to put God first?*

9. *Dare you to share that with someone!*

Truth #3:

Even If You Follow Christ and He is Lord of Your Life, You are Still A Sinner and Always Will Be (and that's okay)

As I closed my eyes one night, I prayed, "God, I've been reading about Abraham. The Bible says things like, 'it was counted to him as righteousness,' and there are other places where people talk about being righteous. I want that. I want to be righteous. Does that mean I don't sin? There are so many things I've stopped doing, places I've stopped sinning in my life, and they were so easy to quit, but there are still so many things I still struggle with! I'm still sinning! I hate that. I don't know how to stop sinning. Am I always going to be a sinner? How do I be righteous? I'll bet I could be righteous in my sleep, when I'm not interacting with anyone, when I'm not dealing with stresses, when I'm just sleeping..." and I remember dozing off around then.

My nights are seldom dream-filled and, when I do have a dream, I don't often remember it. This night, however, I had a dream that is one I still remember as clearly as if it were last night. I'm thankful to say I don't even recognize the evil person I was in my dreams. Somehow, in my sleep,

I donned a black trench coat and black top hat. I then proceeded to lurk in the shadows of a night in an 18th century city. I can remember the cobblestone streets and the clicking of my shoes upon them. I remember the cold, damp air and the steam coming up from grates in the streets as I ran – from one murder to the next. In horrific detail, the night seemed unending. Jack the Ripper seemed to fill my persona. It began when I stole a knife by smashing a store window with a brick and pulled the large blade off a display stand. I remember admiring the white mother-of-pearl handle. Then I heard a man yell, "Hey! You there! And I turned, locked eyes with him, and promptly slit his throat. I lingered, gazing at the pool of crimson seeping into the cracks of the cobblestone underneath his head. He was middle-aged, perhaps around 45, with a grey wool coat. The details of the dream were simply stunning to me. I'm still amazed that I remember them so clearly now. I remember feeling as though I didn't want to do the things I was doing, but could not help it. I remember wishing I would stop being bad, but my hands seemed to have minds of their own and I went from crime to crime. The night's escapades of theft, lies, and assault continued until I somehow realized that I was dreaming. I struggled awake and sat up in bed at 2:11am. I blurted out, "I get it. I am always a sinner, even in my sleep!" Never before, nor since, have I ever experienced nightmares where I was the conduit of evil.

I believe God used that night to clearly make the point to me that without Jesus Christ, I am as depraved as they come. I later combined the experience with my knowledge of the Bible about how we can "squelch" the Holy Spirit through sin and how God sometimes turns even believers over to their sin. Without daily pursuit of Him and the desire to obey, God allows us to have less access to His peace and power.

The good news is, however, that with Jesus Christ we are also saints! And to put your mind at ease, without a doubt, the most powerful thing I've ever learned about faith is that I don't have to work at any of it. If I will but pursue God and obey His teachings, He naturally changes me – and I just start doing the things I'm supposed to do because I'm walking in the Spirit (living rightly, being righteous, whatever you want to call it). It is not a burden. Trusting Him becomes easy and light. It is my prayer to grow such that the place I spend most of my time is in Him.

Let's pause for a moment and take a look at the ugliness of sin in our lives. You may not be ready to go here with me, but if you will, this rocky part of the journey will provide you with a firmer footing on the rest of the path. Until we come face-to-face with our sin and how it separates us from God and from others around us, we will remain stuck in our walk. The depth of our relationships will not change until we confront these things, confess them, and *repent* (turn from sin to new, pure behavior). We will start with the most important commandment for us to obey, that of *love*.

"Teacher, which is the great commandment in the Law?"
And he said to him, "You shall love the Lord your God with
all your heart and with all your soul and with all your mind.
This is the great and first commandment. And the second is
like it: You shall love your neighbor as yourself. On these

two commandments depend all the Law and the Prophets."(Matthew 22:36–40 ESV)

Each missed opportunity to love impacts your relationship with God and others in your life. *"So whoever knows the right thing to do and fails to do it, for him it is sin"* (James 4:17 ESV). Allow yourself to consider for a moment how failing to love God, others, and yourself affects your life.

My greatest sins (that I'm aware of) are fear and pride. These are rooted in a lack of love for God and a lack of love and respect in certain areas for myself and others. Those things are rooted in a lack of consistent time with Him. I struggle with spending time with Him first every single day. Do you? I will often go for five days in a row, then take the entire weekend off. I will attend church, but it is different than having one-on-one time with Him.

And the next thing I know, I'm dealing with fear and pride. In being afraid of what others think, sometimes I resist God, sometimes I am afraid, and other times I emote at the people in my life in unhealthy ways. I have cried over comments people have made about the articles I've written. The "1" and "2" star reviews on Amazon shred my fragile heart when I take them personally. I confess I think those things are about me. Then, my selfishness allows the misinformed, ungodly, and unsaved to wound me when, instead, I should see my work as His work. When I take time to pray and ask for His help in the midst of those moments, He reminds me that it is not all about me and then not only does the pain leave but His compassion and my motivation return.

Sinners Who Love Themselves

Let's go back to Matthew 22:36–40: *"Teacher, which is the great commandment in the Law?" And he said to him, "You shall love the Lord your God with all your heart and with all your soul and with all your mind. This is the great and first commandment. And the second is like it: You shall love your neighbor as yourself. On these two commandments depend all the Law and the Prophets"* (ESV).

What about that part of the verse, *"as yourself?"* If we understand God, we can love ourselves in healthy way – this is different than being selfish. Unfortunately, we live in a culture where secular society denigrates both genders. Take a look at television or magazines with women portrayed as sex objects and men depicted as fools. Our perception of Truth and lies becomes challenging to navigate. Between what the mainstream media communicates and the vast differences among church teachings, a woman can find herself stuck not knowing what to do or how to think about herself even while having the best intentions.

What separates pride and a healthy perception of ourselves as children of the King? Jesus Christ.

Are we placing ourselves first when we make the choice to rest over the many things we could do for others? Do I make some banana bread for my friend battling cancer or do I take a short nap because I'm exhausted? We learn that we are to serve and die to self, but instead we sacrifice our identities on the altar of other people's expectations. How do we figure this out? By choosing to do three things consistently (daily):

1. Learn the Bible (I have hidden Your Word in my heart that I might not sin against You (Psalm 119:11))
2. Obey what we read.
3. Be open to God bringing a verse to mind in the middle of the day – and follow the leading of that verse, asking Him to confirm to you that you are to do so.

I believe the extent to which we have a healthy relationship with ourselves, meaning one not overly indulgent but disciplined, caretaking and encouraging, affects our ability to interact with others, including God, in a more healthy way. Perhaps this is why there is much focus in Christiandom about overcoming our pasts, healing from our hurts, and living in victory. God will heal us from all of our hurts if we will let Him.

How about you?

1. *What is revealed to you as you ponder those verses about loving God and others as ourselves?*

2. *What do you think it means to love yourself?*

3. *Do a little research about Jesus. How did He love Himself?*

4. *How about you? Where do you sin in the "love" category with God? With others? With yourself?*

5. *How would you love a friend well, say if she was upset, hurt, and needed you? What specifically would you do and why would you do it?*

6. *How good of a friend are you to yourself?*

7. *What risk do we run when we do not seek to obey?*

Father, I pray these Truths are from Your hand, may You grow your daughter in wisdom as she learns about Your Great Love. Write down any A-Ha's that you might have in your journal.
Heavenly Father,

I confess my inadequacies in the area of loving You first, and my ability of loving others well, including myself. I have sinned and fallen radically short of Your standards, and I continue to do so daily. I have not fully embraced what You did for me out of love, either.

I do not fully understand the depravity of my spirit and the necessity of Jesus Christ—I confess I am too blinded by the lies of this world to see Your truth completely. Break my heart, oh God that I might weep at the bereft nature of my character. I am thinking specifically of the list of sins, Lord, and the many that I commit and the more that I am blind to. I think of the negative impact these sins have on my relationship with You, and those You've placed in my life. Please forgive me as I take a moment to repent of each of them specifically with You now.

Thank You, Father, for being a God who forgives me through the sacrifice of Jesus Christ. Help me see my need for Your Son more clearly. Help my heart be so full of worship for You that I tremble and shudder at the mere mention of Your name. Help me want to love You first, and, dear God, help me love with Your love.

It's in Jesus' name I pray. Amen.

Be part of our community! You can share what you are doing by emailing us at information@GreaterImpact.org. We will share your action step, using just your first name, with our prayer team.

Truth #4:

The More You Get to Know God, the More You'll See Your Own Sin (and That's Okay)

Dr. Kevin Leman and Shaunti Feldhahn both endorsed *The Respect Dare* in the same week. I was pretty excited. On Saturday night, after receiving the final edits for Dr. Leman's endorsement, I went to bed praying, "Thank You, God, I can't believe You did all this! Please help me stay humble. Don't ever let me think any of this is about me!!" And the next morning, we got up and went to church as a family. The church was one I'd attended since 1999. I'd done Vacation Bible School there every summer for years; participated in Thursday morning Bible study; worked with staff doing training, serving on the personnel committee, teaching classes, and escorting my children to and from their classes when they were little. I had the security code for the alarm system and lock box. To say I was familiar with the building would be a serious understatement.

And the morning I went to church after having prayed for God to keep me humble, I promptly walked right into the men's bathroom.

I stood in the entrance hallway, looked at a young man I knew well washing his hands, and actually had the audacity to think, "Oh, he's in the wrong bathroom!" Then it was, "Why is he washing his hands in here?" Then I thought, "Did they paint in here? It looks different." His eyes kept getting wider – and then I realized I was the one who was in the wrong.

A verse from Proverbs (a book of wisdom in the Bible) popped into my head, "Pride comes before the fall." I remembered that God detests a "haughty spirit" and realized without even trying, I was committing the sin of pride!

I turned and ran out of the bathroom into the hall, right in front of about thirty people I knew. To make matters worse, a friend of mine saw the whole thing, and she said to me, "Nina! What are you doing??!!" and I responded, "Oh, heavens! I don't even know!!" Of course by then, everyone was looking.

I shared with her my prayer from the night before and she laughed her head off at me. We laughed until I had tears in my eyes and I realized God was answering my prayer, keeping me humble.

This ridiculous event makes me smile at the way God answers prayers. He always answers with a "Yes," "No," or "Wait," but we often assume He isn't listening because our listening muscles are weak or distracted with other things. When we begin to see Him everywhere, the Holy Spirit will help us connect the events in our life with verses in the Bible that we have committed to memory and use those things to teach and guide us.

I will share some of my personal journey as we take this brief walk together. I promise we will eventually get to what respect actually looks like but, before that, we need to build a foundation based on truth, hence the title of this book. Our time will be more productive if we study some key Biblical concepts, evaluate our belief system, and then move to a place where we apply what we have learned.

I appreciate your patience with this part of the process. I know you want to get to the application part of respect and learn some tangibles for changing your marriage. But please know I feel deeply led to begin here. Besides, as we were reminded in chapter 1, patience is a virtue and a key element of love[9].

Because our goal is to become more mature in our faith, we need to understand what maturity and immaturity is. Maturity can be defined as having wisdom. That being said, we want to naturally begin in Proverbs. This book of wisdom continues to provide a wealth of information, teaching, perspective, and coaching for me and many other believers. When I learned that the most mature followers of Christ I knew read Proverbs and Psalms daily, I adopted the practice. I read a chapter that corresponds to the day of the month. If today were the twelfth of the month, I would read the entire twelfth chapter of Proverbs. There are thirty-one chapters so wisdom can guide each day of the month if we let it. I've been doing this for over ten years and still learn something with every single daily reading. Adding five Psalms a day (there are one hundred and fifty) helps us develop compassion for

---

[9] 1 Corinthians 5:8-13

others and enriches our prayers. I believe Billy Graham first made the practice public, but it is one that is common to people who want to continue growing their relationship with God. This does not mean we stop reading the rest of the Bible, however. Depending on the season of life you are in, sometimes it helps to just have your Bible open on the counter all day. I remember when my kids were little, it would sometimes take all day just to get through Proverbs! Do what you can do, knowing God will bless any effort you put towards growing your relationship with Him.

"The fear of the Lord is the beginning of knowledge, but fools despise wisdom and discipline" (Proverbs 1:7 NIV).

Mature wives revere God in such a way that they are willing to obey His Word in the Bible regardless of the suffering or sacrifice involved. Immature wives want what they want instead, usually for their own pleasure. I have been both, by the way, and sometimes still struggle with issues of immaturity. The biggest area of contrast for me, however, shows up in the areas of affection and romance. As a young and immature wife, I wanted these things from my husband because they would make me feel better about myself.

Now that I wrap my identity up in God's opinion of me, I still desire affection and romance in my marriage, but this desire has nothing to do with me and my sense of self. The interesting thing is my desire for them is to help my husband feel more connected and for our kids to see what marriage could look like when two people love each other well.

The following list represents some character traits of immature behavior and thoughts that are described in Proverbs and other parts of the Bible. The opposite of them is maturity and they are represented multiple times in the Bible in various ways. Go slowly through these. Allow the Lord time to speak to you. Please also know that I still have many of my own moments of immaturity, but I deeply desire to become a mature Christian woman in everything I do and I choose to stay on the journey with you.

Write the opposite, positive and mature characteristic next to each of the below. The first is done for you.

Immature Behavior shows up when we are:

1. Impatient   ___*Patient*_____

"A person's wisdom yields patience; it is to one's glory to overlook an offense." (Proverbs 19:11 NIV)

2. Prideful   _____

"When pride comes, then comes disgrace, but with humility comes wisdom." (Proverbs 11:2 NIV)

3. Easily angered   _____

"A wise man is cautious and turns from evil, but a fool is easily angered and is careless." (Proverbs 14:16 HCSB)

4. Short tempered   _____

"People with understanding control their anger; a hot temper shows great foolishness." (Proverbs 14:29 NLT)

5. Lazy _____

"Lazy hands make for poverty, but diligent hands bring wealth." (Proverbs 10:4 NIV)

6. Starting an argument _____

"Starting a quarrel is like breaching a dam; so drop the matter before a dispute breaks out." (Proverbs 17:14 NIV)

7. Disagreeable _____

"A quarrelsome wife is as annoying as a constant dripping on a rainy day." (Proverbs 27:15 NLT)

8. Hating being corrected or disciplined

_____

"He who is often reproved, yet stiffens his neck, will suddenly be broken beyond healing." (Proverbs 29:1 ESV)

9. Not wanting advice from others

_____

"The way of a fool is right in his own eyes, but a wise man listens to advice." (Proverbs 12:15 NIV)

10. Rejecting guidance _____

"Let the wise hear and increase in learning, and the one who understands obtain guidance." (Proverbs 1:5 ESV)

11. Talking too much _____

"When words are many transgression is not lacking, but whoever restrains his lips is prudent." (Proverbs 10:19 ESV)

12. Thinking we are wise _____

"Do you see a person wise in their own eyes? There is more hope for a fool than for them." (Proverbs 26:12 NIV)

13. Having close friends who are foolish

"Whoever walks with the wise becomes wise, but the companion of fools will suffer harm." (Proverbs 13:20 ESV)

14. Not giving to the needy
"One gives freely, yet grows all the richer, another withholds what he should give, and only suffers want." (Proverbs 11:24 ESV)

15. Harshly defending against another person's anger

"A gentle answer turns away wrath, but a harsh word stirs up anger." (Proverbs 15:1 NIV)

16. Constantly giving opinions or interrupting others

"A fool finds no pleasure in understanding but delights in airing his own opinions." (Proverbs 18:2 NIV)

17. Bragging
"Let another praise you, and not your own mouth; someone else, and not your own lips." (Proverbs 27:2 NIV)

18. Listening only to people who say what we want to hear or rejecting truth from others

"So as iron sharpens iron, so one person sharpens another." (Proverbs 27:17)
"Wounds from a friend can be trusted, but an enemy multiplies kisses." (Proverbs 27:6 NIV)

19. Loving to argue _____

"It is an honor for a man to keep aloof from strife, but every fool will be quarreling." (Proverbs 20:3 ESV)

20. Answering before listening – interrupting
_____

"He who answers before listening—that is his folly and his shame." (Proverbs 18:13)

21. Annoyed quickly _____
"A fool shows his annoyance at once, but a prudent man overlooks an insult." (Proverbs 12:16 NIV)

22. Nagging _____
"It's better to live alone in the desert than with a quarrelsome, complaining wife." (Proverbs 21:19 ESV)

23. Showing little mercy _____
"Whoever oppresses the poor shows contempt for their Maker, but whoever is kind to the needy honors God." (Proverbs 14:31 NIV)

24. Speaking without thinking
_____

"He who guards his lips guards his life, but he who speaks rashly will come to ruin." (Proverbs 13:3 NIV)

25. Not fearing God _____
"The fear of the LORD is instruction in wisdom, and humility comes before honor." (Proverbs 15:33 ESV)
26. Seeking revenge _____
"Do not say, 'I'll pay you back for this wrong!' Wait for the Lord, and He will deliver you." (Proverbs 20:22 NIV)

27. Lacking self-control _____

"A person without self-control is like a city with broken-down walls." (Proverbs 25:28 NLT)

28. Seeking riches _____

"Don't wear yourself out trying to get rich. Be wise enough to know when to quit." (Proverbs 23:4 NLT)

29. Saying negative things about others

_____

"Whoever covers an offense seeks love, but he who repeats a matter separates close friends." (Proverbs 17:9 ESV)

30. Being afraid _____

"You need not be afraid of sudden disaster or the destruction that comes upon the wicked." (Proverbs 3:25 NLT)

31. Lying _____

"Truthful words stand the test of time, but lies are soon exposed." (Proverbs 12:19 NLT)

32. Betraying confidences/stirring up trouble by gossip

_____

"A deceitful man stirs dissension, and anyone who gossips separates friends." (Proverbs 16:28 ESV)

33. Lacking discretion   _____

"Like a gold ring in a pig's snout is a beautiful woman without discretion." (Proverbs 11:22 ESV)

34. Discontent   _____

"Better to have little, with fear for the Lord, than to have great treasure and inner turmoil." (Proverbs 15:16 NLT)

35. Ridiculing instruction   _____

"Whoever loves discipline loves knowledge, but one who hates correction is stupid." (Proverbs 12:1)

36. Unknowingly destroying their lives with their own words and actions (or lack of actions)

_____

"A wise woman builds her home, but a foolish woman tears it down with her own hands." (Proverbs 14:1 NLT)

I want to caution you as you reflect. Too many women are in abusive relationships. Too many women also are domineering and/or controlling in their marriages. The same is true for men. I pray, as you walk through responding, that God reveals to you the truth of your situation. If you are controlling and manipulative, you may be tempted to view yourself more favorably than you should. If you are insecure or abused, you may view yourself too harshly. It might help you to secure the assistance of a good friend in reflecting if you do not sense God's perspective in these things.

Above all, be open to whatever truth He reveals to you. The book of Proverbs is not the only place where wisdom and maturity are contrasted with foolishness. Descriptions of foolish sin exist throughout the entire Bible. Here are a few more potential opportunities for growth in terms of identifying Biblical sin. I first saw a list like this in Pastor James MacDonald's excellent work, *Downpour*[10]. It had a profound effect on me as I read through it. The idea stuck with me and I added to it over time, changing it to include many commonly known opportunities for growth that we are familiar with in Christiandom. As you go through the list:

- Slowly, prayerfully consider each one
- Think through the incidents in which these things manifest in your behavior
- Consider the short term AND the long term effects of them in terms of how they impact others
- Stay focused on your own issues
- Resist the urge to point the finger of judgment at anyone else in your life, particularly your husband
- Put a check next to those that you have issues with

As you go through the lists, you may be feeling flames of resentment toward your husband licking at your heart. His sin may be screaming off the pages while your wounded heart yearns for healing. You may be tempted to point a finger at him and his lack of maturity because the lists do not apply only to women, but to all people who follow Christ. You also may feel defensive when you come across one that represents an area of immaturity/foolishness within yourself.

---

[10] James MacDonald, Downpour, LifeWay Press, 2006

Before you begin, take a moment to remember that even Christ did not come to judge the world[11] and that this temptation to judge yourself or others with a "better than" or critical spirit is sin. The Bible also tells us that we will be judged with the same standard which we judge others. Therefore be mindful, but be open to whatever God would reveal to you as you go through these:

Disregards boundaries
Addiction
Occult involvement
Allowing harm to others
Attention seeking
Bigotry
Profanity
Boisterous
Coercive
Controlling
Must repay kindness
Contemptuous
Critical
Defiant
Defensive
Prejudice
Disobedient
Disrespectful
Self-justification
Domineering attitude
Drunkenness
Failing to speak up
Unjust

Failing to care for
   physical self
Failing to build others up
False guilt
Conceit
Feeling helpless
Fearful
White lies
Feeling stupid
Gluttonous
Greediness
Sexual lust
Sexually deviant
Idolatry
Insecurity
Judgmental
Keeping a list of wrongs
Loner
Manipulative
Materialistic
Need to be right
Obsessive
Oppressive

---

[11] John 3:17 (NASB) For God did not send the Son into the world to judge the world, but that the world might be saved through Him.

Overly sensitive to
criticism
Perfectionism
Rebellion to authority
Resentment
Anxiety
Self-confidence
Self-hatred
Self-reliance
Sexual immorality
Vanity
Bitterness
Bossiness
Controlled by peer
pressure
Depression
Disdain
Drug dependency
False modesty
Feeling rejected
Feeling worthless
Hatred
Hostility
Impure thoughts
Intemperance
Low self-esteem

Murder
Negativism
Opinionated
Overly quiet
Passivity
Projecting blame
Refuse to forgive
Rejecting
Restlessness
Self-centeredness
Self-harming
Self-pity
Self-righteousness
Sensuality
Stubbornness
Too talkative
Theft
Un-humble
Unloving
Untruthful
Weak
Withholding intimacy –
Physical or relational
Workaholic

Be patient. We will deal with what to do when your husband sins against you later. For now, if you felt yourself tempted to focus on his behavior, go back over the list again, completing the exercise with your eyes focused on your own behavior. Be objective and careful not to categorize your behavior incorrectly. If you are someone who is controlled by others or a people pleaser, you might have a tendency to view yourself in ways that are not healthy. Ask God to reveal His truth to you. If you are one who is controlling or manipulative of others, you may not see this. Ask a good friend for help if you need to.

Perhaps some on the list stood out to you. In prayer, review the list again and ask God to reveal the top three areas for you to focus on. Circle those.

Strong, mature women of faith are not intimidated or threatened by authority, even when that authority is poorly handled or wielded over them. A wise and mature wife recognizes that her husband's sinful behavior speaks volumes about his walk with God, *as her response to his behavior speaks to hers*. She is not afraid of following a man who is still figuring himself out. She recognizes that she may be dealing with immaturity and responds accordingly, the way Christ would, with truth, love, compassion, and patience, and sometimes confrontation. She knows she has enough of her own issues to keep her focused for a lifetime. Stay focused on what we are doing now so you don't miss the benefits. Remember Jesus in the Garden on the night before He was crucified. He let the disciples know they had disappointed Him (He was truthful) but He also saw them where they were in their walk, knowing that their spirits were willing, but their flesh was weak. They were tired. He asked for what He needed from them. They let Him down and He communicated about it.

The book of Proverbs in the Bible helps us understand that within each of us are three people:[12]

---

[12] Dr. Henry Cloud, "Necessary Endings," Harper Collins Christian Publishing, 2010.

1. The wise man
2. The foolish man
3. The evil man

If we are dealing with an area of wisdom, we can know this by recognizing our response to feedback. We welcome it, and will offer apology if someone corrects us or the feedback is negative. We then will change our behavior.

If we are defensive, we are operating out of an area within us that is foolish and immature. We justify our behavior, make excuses, blame others, become angry, etc. We do not change our behavior because we alter reality to fit the truth we believe instead of responding in wisdom. If we don't care that we hurt someone or are aware that we intended to hurt them, we are operating out of an evil part of our heart.

How we deal with these areas within ourselves and others matters. If we see correction within an area of wisdom, the correct response is repentance – apology and behavior adjustment. If someone else's request for us is out of line, we still understand their perspective of how they've been wronged, and we still apologize. We then will work through win/win or simply repent with behavior change.

If dealing with an area of foolishness (which is simply a high level of immaturity), the only response that "works" is to set limits and allow natural consequences. If our sin is gluttony, for example, joining an accountability group for weight management would be helpful. Having a friend hold us accountable once a week would be helpful. Setting limits around the types of food you will buy and the amount of exercise you will engage in also will help. Setting up rewards and consequences for goal achievement- based on movement toward or away from goals will help. For example, a new pair of jeans for positive movement towards goals or losing a night of eating out for negative movement away from goals.

If we are dealing with an area of evil in our hearts, only time in the Bible and seeking God's work in our lives will help. The Holy Spirit will convict us of our sin and we can move forward. While we should be careful in judging others, these three people are in all of us and the way we treat them is the same as the way we would deal with ourselves. You can tell if you are married to a wise man if he receives feedback from you and apologizes, then changes his behavior. A fool will be defensive, angry, argumentative, justify his behavior, and not change. You may have to set limits and allow natural consequences, depending on the impact and the area of foolishness. At the time of this writing, we are working on Daughters of Sarah Part 3, which will address how to deal with these different people in a marriage.

Now that you have your top three areas of immaturity, write them down in your journal, and, next to each, write the effect these sins have on your marriage, your husband, your relationship with God, and yourself.
Take some time to process this with God directing your steps.
1. Ask God to forgive you for sinning in these areas and for the hurt you have caused. Be specific.
2. Ask God to help you change, to turn from your sinful ways.
3. Ask God for His strength.
4. Ask God to reveal to you what you need to do when you are about to sin.

5. Listen closely and make notes about what God reveals to you. Remember He will always show you a way out of sin—your job is to take it.
6. Thank God for what He is about to do in your life.

How About You?

1. *How did the brief discussion about wisdom and maturity affect you?* Perhaps you are unable to move past the hurt you feel caused by the hands of others. To truly focus on your own sin and behaviors, you must get past that hurt. If this is you, know that it is a common issue. We cannot really repent of our own behavior until we see it the way God does.

2. It might help you to make a list of the things your husband has done to hurt you, the sins he has committed against you. Write down how each thing made you feel. Then, set this aside and go back and work your way through the exercise again, focusing on your own sins.

After you make your list about your husband, you have two choices. One, you can choose in your heart to forgive your husband without interacting with him over it. This means you simply forgive him and let God deal with it. When situations arise in the future, you address them at that time. Two, you can show him the list and tell him you are hurting over these things and that you need him to listen to you, apologize and let you say you forgive him. If you choose the second option, realize he may not want to do this. In fact, it might cause more conflict, but this can be a good thing, especially if you have a counselor or lay marriage mentors helping you. If you begin with your own apology first communicating how you think you've hurt him and then deeply empathizing with his feelings, he might be open to hearing your hurts. In either case, do what you sense God would have you do and then change your behavior.

Repentance is behavioral change. It is mature Christianity and a daily part of a believer's journey.

1. *How have you defined mature and immature behavior in the past? How is your perception of your current circumstances affected by what you have learned here?*

2. *What characteristics of a mature Christian wife used to come to mind? Is that different now? What will you do differently as a result?*

Chapter Dare:

Recall the last time you sinned in each of those top three areas. Write out for each, step by step, what happened in order and determine where you will stop next time. I urge you to select a spot that is as far away as possible from the sin actually occurring. Often by the time we get close, it is too late and we are too weak. Paul tells us to run from sin. This is one way we can do that. Be clear with yourself where you are "drawing the line." Pray and ask God for His guidance and His help as you do this exercise.

1. Consider who you have hurt because of your sin. In the next chapter, you'll learn more about apologizing well. Who do you need to send a note to or have a one-on-one conversation with that you have hurt?

2. Forgive yourself. That means you cannot rub these sins in your own face and demean yourself with them. Keep no list of wrongs against yourself. Do not allow shame or guilt to discourage you. Practice taking every thought captive and give those shameful and guilt-ridden thoughts to God. Refuse to allow the enemy even a tiny bit of your time. You are forgiven.[13] Comfort yourself by these steps:

   a. Acknowledge the feeling and name it
   b. Be a good friend to yourself by validating and normalizing your feelings. Remind yourself that anyone would feel like this. Make sure you understand as many nuances of how you feel and why before moving on to the next step.
   c. Comfort yourself physically to release oxytocin by rubbing your arms, putting your hands on your chest, or hugging yourself.
   d. Find the good in the situation and thank God for allowing things to occur the way they did.
   e. Speak a gentle and encouraging word of truth to yourself, seeing another person's point of view, and/or God's.

3. Recall the three areas of sin. What will be different in your life when God grows you in holiness in these? Be as specific as possible:

4. Praise God for what He is about to do.

---

[13] 1 John 1:9 (NASB) If we confess our sins, He is faithful and righteous to forgive us our sins and to cleanse us from all unrighteousness.

A mature Christian woman has a teachable spirit and enthusiastically and passionately pursues God's lessons. Discipline and correction are welcome friends to her as are the wise thoughts and advice of others. She is humble, patient, long-suffering and perseverant. She sees each difficulty as an opportunity to learn, even if her behavior did not cause the trouble. She works hard and is not idle. She is brave and confident in her God, regardless of whether times are good or bad. She takes care of her family and does not embarrass them by her behavior. She speaks highly of her husband and children. She works hard, whether inside the home or out. She is generous to those with less.

A mature Christian woman is clothed with strength and dignity and has a positive outlook on life, smiling at the days to come. All these things are true because she puts her faith, hope, and trust in God alone. Her identity is defined by what the Audience of One thinks of her, and her efforts are for pleasing Him alone.

Truth #5:

Building Friendship within Your Marriage – even when it is hard – is Worth It

During a difficult time in our marriage, my husband and I finally shared some of our past hurts with each other. I remember how surprised I was when I learned my mountain-of-a-man deeply needed my presence as he went through life. Married five years before birthing our first child, we developed a deep friendship by exploring the world together, going to art and antique shows, camping, and driving around on various adventures on the weekend. As the babies came, I grew more and more desperate for solitude and time away, so I encouraged my husband, Jim, to explore and do things with the kids. I frequently stayed home.

Most marriages go through a period like this, with couples experiencing a drop-off in marital satisfaction when children arrive.

Ours were still at home when Jim shared with me about how he missed my company. I had thought that since we were still dating each other, that those times counted. In his mind, however, the dates were nice but they were not activities one would do with a friend. He experiences love by doing things with me and I needed to carve out more time to make sure he felt loved by me in this way.

Decades of research by Gottman,[14] (who can predict with 96 percent accuracy whether or not a couple will divorce from just five minutes of watching them) indicate that a solid friendship is key to the success of a marriage. His research also indicates that specific communication behaviors add to the destruction of a marriage.

Clear advice to married couples also is presented in the book of Ephesians:

"Therefore a man shall leave his father and mother and hold fast to his wife, and the two shall become one flesh." This mystery is profound, and I am saying that it refers to Christ and the church. *However, let each one of you love his wife as himself, and let the wife see that she respects her husband.* (Ephesians 5:31–33 ESV, emphasis added)

I wondered what Christ had to say to this church regarding His relationship with her and found this:

To the Church in Ephesus
*"To the angel of the church in Ephesus write: 'The words of him who holds the seven stars in his right hand, who walks among the seven golden lampstands. "*I know your works, your toil and your patient endurance, and how you cannot bear with those who are evil, but have tested those who call themselves apostles and are not, and found them to be false. I know you are enduring patiently and bearing up for my name's sake, and you have not grown weary. But I have this against you that you have abandoned the love you had at first. Remember therefore from where you have fallen; repent, and do the works you did at first. *If*

---

[14] The Seven Principles for Making Marriage Work, John M. Gottman, Ph.D., and Nan Silver

not, I will come to you and remove your lampstand from its place, unless you repent. Yet this you have: you hate the works of the Nicolaitans, which I also hate. He who has an ear, let him hear what the Spirit says to the churches. To the one who conquers I will grant to eat of the tree of life, which is in the paradise of God.' (Revelation 2:1–7 ESV, emphasis mine)

What did we do at first in our relationships with our husbands? Most of us pursued that important friendship. We were sincerely interested in the guy we married. We put effort into spending time with him, getting to know him, deeply loving him. God wired us to pursue this relationship, to persevere, and we have toiled and endured. Let us not abandon our love for our husband (or our God) and the passionate enthusiasm we had in the beginning. It is likely that if you are not doing the things you did at first, your husband misses them whether he is aware of this or not.

A friend lamented after her youngest child left home after college that she did not know who she was any more. Her large house was empty. She told me she felt her voice echo against nothingness. Her husband traveled extensively for work and she did not know what to do with her time. "I used to be someone," she told me one day. "I just can't remember who."

In serving her family well for all those years, she forgot to take care of her relationship with herself and her relationship with her husband. When he is home, they sit in separate rooms surfing the Internet and shopping. I pray she finds the girl she used to be soon. Unfortunately, the empty nest is one of the times when marital satisfaction plummets and the divorce rate spikes.

Couples who have failed to invest in their marriages while the children were at home forget who they are as a couple when the children are gone. A consistent investment in your marriage while your children are at home reaps benefits for the entire family. They learn what a loving relationship looks like and how important marriage is to both of you. You and your husband invest in a relationship that withstands difficulties, thereby strengthening it.

Did you also see the word, *repent,* in the text from Revelation 2:5? Often the fastest way to jumpstart your relationships with God and your husband is to apologize for how you have hurt him by not doing the things you used to do together. If you then invite him to start doing the things you used to do as a couple (or similar ones), usually he will happily join you. If you find the thought of this as challenging as I did the first time I tried it that is probably the sin of pride rearing its ugly head.

In the first five years of our marriage, I accompanied my husband on the weekends and in the evenings on plenty of adventures. When I realized that my participation in these activities had dwindled over the years after the children arrived, I was faced with a dilemma. I had early-onset arthritis thanks to a connective tissue disorder and spending long hours walking around or sitting in a car were unpleasant, at the very least. I had to wrestle with God first to align my heart with His, and then ask Him to help me be a better friend to my husband.

Then I talked with Jim about it. I asked what he missed about the early days of our marriage. I listened. I apologized for hurting him. He forgave me. I promised to work on this, asking him how I could meet his need of companionship in a better way. I brought up the concerns I had with my physical condition and we worked out some solutions. He understood more about me and vice-versa, and we were on the way to doing the things "we did at first," in a fresh and creative new way. It was good for our marriage.

Notice that even though it seemed I had a good reason to not be a better companion to Jim, it still hurt him. Apologies are sometimes just a step in healing—not always are they a confession of wronging someone by our sin. Sometimes we hurt someone inadvertently, through no fault of our own. However, we can still say, "I'm so sorry you are hurting. You must have felt very lonely for a long time (or whatever they felt—it's called empathy and it is the salve to healing relationship damage) and it grieves me to know you have been suffering for so long. I am really sorry. Will you forgive me?"

Sometimes we may receive an apology from our spouse for hurts he has caused us. We must follow God's advice and forgive. This is another way of being mature in Christ, by extending His grace to another.

Refusing to forgive when we have been hurt by someone is like trying to take revenge by drinking poison and expecting the other person to die. Forgive yourself, too, and then move on so your relationships can begin to heal. Remember what God says to us about apologies and forgiveness:

> *Therefore, if you are offering your gift at the altar and there remember that your brother has something against you, leave your gift there in front of the altar. First go and be reconciled to your*

brother; then come and offer your gift. (Matthew 5:23–24 NIV)

Then Peter came to Jesus and asked, "Lord, how many times shall I forgive my brother when he sins against me? Up to seven times?" Jesus answered, "I tell you, not seven times, but seventy-seven times." (Matthew 18:21–22 NIV)

And when you stand praying, if you hold anything against anyone, forgive him, so that your Father in heaven may forgive you your sins. (Mark 11:25 NIV)

Notice that we are to initiate reconciliation whether we hold something against someone else or they hold it against us! And clearly, God does not even want our worship until we have apologized for sinning against someone. Any time we behave unlovingly or disrespectfully, we are committing sin. We also are to forgive others, even when they do not apologize. Harboring unforgiveness eats away at our souls and makes us bitter. Apologies to others and grace given via forgiveness (especially from God) are salve to wounds. Many marriages will simply not move forward without them. *And yes, we will talk about how to handle things when he sins against you; and, yes, I know he has hurt you deeply as well—but you cannot change his behavior. You can only control your own and the way you respond.*

It may take a while for your husband to willingly work on your marriage or to forgive you, but if you persevere God will eventually soften his heart toward you. During this time, it is important to remember that your God is your best husband:

For your Maker is your husband, the LORD of hosts is his name; and the Holy One of Israel is your Redeemer, the God of the whole earth he is called. (Isaiah 54:5 ESV)

It also should not shock you that some of the advice from the more mature women in the Bible to the younger ones is to be "friends" of their husbands. In the following verse, *love* translates as *phileo*-love which means "friendship-love." We are told by God to do this ourselves, and we need to encourage young wives to be their husbands' friends.

Titus 2:3-5 (ESV) *3 Older women likewise are to be reverent in behavior, not slanderers or slaves to much wine. They are to teach what is good, 4 and so train the young women to love their husbands and children, 5 to be self-controlled, pure, working at home, kind, and submissive to their own husbands, that the word of God may not be reviled.* (Titus 2:3–5 ESV)

How about You?

1. *What choice will you make today? Who will you follow? What is God placing on your heart now?*

2. *What has stood in the way of moving forward in the area of reconciliation for you?*

3. *How have you dealt with that in the past?*

4. *What do you need to do differently?*

Chapter Dares:

In an effort to begin building or deepening your relationship with your husband, we are offering you these dares. You will continue these through the rest of the book and, hopefully, keep them after you are finished here with us! This is considered "Friendship 101."

It is likely that your husband needs you to be his best friend. This is true for about 85 percent of the men out there. Our husbands need to be able to get honest feedback from us and will need help at times of great importance because, as Proverbs 27:6 tells us, *Wounds from a friend can be trusted. But an enemy kisses you many times.* Satan wants you to be at odds with each other instead of friends. He wants you either to be prideful and domineering or to be a doormat. If you are humbly strong, like Christ, this changes everything.

Your husband needs a friend he can confide in, trust deeply, and work through issues with. Praise God if he has some excellent male friends in his life. Even so, according to Christian family therapist Dr. Kevin Leman, your husband deeply desires one of those confidants to be you. You will have times when he will need to hear you dish some hard truth lovingly his way; things no one else loves him enough to say. Having said that, until he trusts that you are fully on his side, fully in his corner, fully his best friend, he cannot hear any of these things from you.

The dares in this chapter begin the process of moving you and your husband closer together. More importantly, however, they begin your steps in deeply obeying God's Word to wives in the Bible.

Dare 1: Apologize to God and your husband (and anyone else you have hurt) for sinning against them. *Spend some time in prayer, confessing and asking God to help you "do the things you did at first" in your marriage. Know He forgives you. Write your husband a short note specifically apologizing for not being a better friend. Tell him you are sorry you have sinned against him and that you want to do better. Ask him to forgive you. Put the note on the steering wheel of his car or in his underwear drawer.*

A great apology typically begins with, "I'm so sorry I . . ." and speaks to empathize about the affect your behavior may have had.

For example, saying "I'm so sorry I came across that way to you. I can tell I've upset you and I'm really sorry about that," is radically different from saying "I'm so sorry you don't understand what I said."

Empathize with the person—"How did it make you feel? ... I think I've felt similarly when (tell short story about a hurt of yours that does NOT involve them)... I'm so sorry to have impacted you like this..."

Take ownership for the pain you caused – "I was wrong." Set an expectation for change—"I'll do everything in my power not to do that again."

Ask forgiveness—"Will you please forgive me?"

Inquire as to how you can restore the situation – "What can I do to make this up to you?"

Dare 2: Sit down with your husband and make a list of the things you did in the beginning of your marriage. You

might even start an "Our Favorite Memories" list on your refrigerator for your family with a special section titled, "Just the Two of Us." *If you have young children, they will love doing this. Teens tend to think this is a weird exercise. You might engage them by asking them around the dinner table, "What's the most fun thing we've ever done together as a family?" and let the discussion flow, putting them on the poster yourself.*

- *Discuss your list with your husband. Ask him which of the things on the list are ones he misses the most and why. Listen. Invite him to do those with you (or something similar if there's a reason you can't do them now). If your husband will not make the list, ask God to reveal them to you.*
- *If you put the memories list on the refrigerator, add a few details about something the two of you did together when dating or during your marriage that was fun for both of you, adding to the list once a week.*

As you read through the above dares, do any of them seem extra hard to you? Why or why not?

If you are doing this with a small group, what do you need prayer for? Write out your prayer requests in your journal, and then share them with your group when you meet:

Truth #6:

If You Feed Your Heart, Mind, and Soul More Secular Media Than Biblical Truth, You Will Come to Believe Many Lies

Leaning on the marble counter in my friend's kitchen, chatting away, I jumped as her husband swore loudly. Dog toenails racing across hardwood followed the loud, "yelp!" Their young dog sped around the corner to hide behind the protective legs of my friend. Her husband stormed into the room, seemed startled at the sight of me, then said, "Excuse me," and turned around and left hiding something.

I looked at my friend inquisitively. She turned, called the dog, and let him out into the backyard. I noticed a shock collar around the dog's neck. Her husband must have zapped the dog.

"Mickey's in training," she said.

"Oh," I said. "How's that going?"

"Um, not very well," she replied, and changed the subject.

Sitting in Sunday school classes and listening to innumerable Bible teachers talk about all the verses in the Bible related to being a wife left me feeling like that dog.

Emotional, mental, and nearly physical "shocks" zapped my culturally influenced sense of self as the teacher talked about submission, respect, and not denying each other (in the bedroom). I remember being furious—at whom, I was not sure—but, nevertheless, anger coursed through my veins, fed by a wounded heart. I felt lied to and deceived.

What I did not realize at the time was that the resentment and anger was God's Word colliding with my perception of truth. It actually indicated a serious lack of maturity in my spiritual walk. I grew up feeding myself the lies of the culture – don't worry, be happy; have it my way; have it all; I'm a good person, etc. My natural, sinful nature did not want to accept what I am: a sinner. A sinner who does not like the thought of submitting to anyone, not the other human I married—and even less, God. I thought submission meant that my husband is better than me. I wondered if God loved men more than women. I struggled.

Bigger than my lack of understanding of my nature, pride ruled my heart. It angered me that I could not be good and "do right" on my own. Within us, God may have wired a desire to be good (or that desire might be His Spirit), but the *actual ability to be good* only comes through the Holy Spirit. We often ignore the Spirit's leading in a brief moment in the middle of an interaction. Instead, we take the easy (short term, for us) way out and justify our behavior, then judge and blame the other person, committing more sins. James 4:17 (NIV) tells us that if we know what is good and do not do it, we are sinning. For example's sake, let's talk about toilet paper. If I use the last bit on the roll and do not put up a new one, I am choosing (in a very small way) to not listen to the Holy Spirit. If I have the thought, "I should replace the roll," and do not, I might then be tempted to think something that then justifies my lack of obedience to what is right. I might judge myself, saying, "I'm so lazy anyway, why should I change, I can't be different anyway;" or I justify my actions while I judge my husband or kids by thinking, "I'm always the one doing all the work, let them deal with the outcome – see how they like it." Either approach is sin because we've ignored the Holy Spirit's prompting. Not only have we missed an opportunity to be used by God in the small things, but we have actually architected a state of being in our own hearts that creates more of what we don't want – to either feel bad about ourselves or to think others don't care for us. I believe this is one of the reasons the Bible tells us in Luke 16:10 that if we can be trusted in the small things then we can be trusted in the bigger ones.

Without the Spirit's intervention, we do and say the wrong things because we choose to listen to our own desires and because we are more easily influenced by the enemy than we realize. We also often forget these things and think that because we have conquered one area of sin we are free in all areas. Maybe we have had victory and no longer commit the sin of drunkenness, but then we boast about how long we have stayed sober without giving God the credit and commit the sin of pride. We spend a lot of time judging one sin as not as bad as another, forgetting two things: 1) *all* sin separates us from God,[15] and 2) ironically,

---

[15] 1 John 5:17a (NIV) All wrongdoing is sin

judgment is itself a sin![16] We forget that our husband also is a sinner, and expecting him to be perfect, we judge him too.

We are wired to worship *something* and we will worship the wrong things if not daily pursuing obedience to and worship of God. The sad truth is that we wander off; it is just so easy. Evidences of this are seen daily in the newspaper accounts of "good Christian people," leaders, even, who succumb to the worship of wealth. Pastors succumb to the lure of power and become prideful, leaving broken congregations in their wake. Affairs, tax evasion, embezzlement, child abuse, divorce, pornography addiction, and substance abuse are only a few of the public sins we are made aware of as God's "good people" fall. And we often forget that we are not any different than these public figures, only our sins are not as public.

Hang on, we will get some encouragement in a minute.

While we are as quick to rush into judgment of the public figures around us leading imperfect lives as we are to condemn other "sinners" (murderers, child abusers, thieves, rapists, liars, pedophiles, and the like), we need to remember that *we are the same as* all *of them, Christian or otherwise. The only difference between us and "the unsaved sinners" is we have accepted what Jesus did for all His people and we have the gift of hope. There also is no difference between us and "the other Christians" who have also accepted His gift of salvation.* I'm not differentiating between "carnal" Christians and others simply because everyone's journey starts in different ways. Some have a

---

[16] Romans 2:1 (NIV) ... you who pass judgment on someone else, for at whatever point you judge the other, you are condemning yourself, because you who pass judgment do the same things.

huge conversion moment and are different immediately. Others do not, and their rate of growth is slower.

I realize that thought might be discouraging. But I also am still very much a sinner.

There is tremendous freedom and hope in acknowledging the fact that to be in communion with God, we always will need daily what Christ did for us.

We like to judge one another's sin in the Christian community because, immature in our understanding of who we are in Christ, this judgment helps us feel better about ourselves. We like to label one sin as worse because it is an "abomination" or because "God hates" it. We pat ourselves on the backs, saying, "Well, at least I am not a [murderer, adulterer, etc.]," in a futile effort to build up who we are at the expense of someone else. We soon will be discussing how to know who we are in Christ and the victory that comes with that. But for now, we simply need to wrap our brains around Paul's truth:

Therefore you have no excuse, everyone of you who passes judgment, for in that which you judge another, you condemn yourself; for you who judge practice the same things. And we know that the judgment of God rightly falls upon those who practice such things. (Romans 2:1–2 NAS)

What then? Are we better than they? Not at all; for we have already charged that both Jews and Greeks are all under sin; as it is written, "There is none righteous, not even one." (Romans 3:9–10 NAS)

Even Paul, the great leader himself, lamented about his own sin nature:

For we are conscious that the law is of the spirit; but I am of the flesh, given into the power of sin. And I have no clear knowledge of what I am doing, for that which I have a mind to do, I do not, but what I have a hate for, that I do. . . . For I am conscious that in me, that is, in my flesh, there is nothing good; I have the mind but not the power to do what is right. For the good which I have a mind to do, I do not; but the evil which I have no mind to do, that I do. . . . I give praise to God through Jesus Christ our Lord. So with my mind I am a servant to the law of God, but with my flesh to the law of sin. (Romans 7:14–15, 18–19, 25 BBE, emphasis mine)

If this mighty man of God understood the nature of his flesh to be sinful, *who are we to think we are good*? At first glance, this may sound like a tremendously discouraging thought. After meditating upon it, however, can you see why this, too, actually is very encouraging?

Think about it.

Think about the last sinful thing you did that comes to mind. Was it the "little white lie" you told so you did not have to run carpool? Maybe it was blaming one of the kids for the mess you left in the kitchen? Maybe you let your thoughts wander a little too far after reading that romantic novel? Perhaps you were watching worship music on the Internet and that sidebar had some really tantalizing videos on it and you went ahead and watched? Maybe you compared your husband to someone else's and longed for yours to be different? No one knew you did it, so it does not count, right? All sin has consequences.[17] And God sees all of it. *The more we come to know Christ, the more we realize how very black our hearts really are.*

So why should this encourage us?

Knowing that we are the same as every person we come in contact with, regardless of what they have done or what we have done, provides victory and freedom from judgment. It provides us with a basis for healthy confidence. We can look at others and realize that if they are judging or condemning our behavior (or someone else's) they are simply immature in their walk with God. We also are immature if we are judging the behavior of others. Even if we are not committing the same sin as someone else, we are not free to judge that person because we then are committing sin ourselves. Even Jesus Christ said He did not come to judge the world.[18] The Biblical truth is that "sin is sin"[19] to God, "All have sinned and fall short of the glory of God,"[20] helps us understand three things:

1. Those who criticize and condemn us are committing the sin of judgment.
2. We can actively recognize their sin of judgment and choose to not accept their condemnation[21]

---

[17] Galatians 6:8 (NIV) The one who sows to please his sinful nature, from that nature will reap destruction; the one who sows to please the Spirit, from the Spirit will reap eternal life.

[18] John 3:17 (ESV) For God did not send his Son into the world to condemn the world, but in order that the world might be saved through him.

[19] 1 John 5:17a (ESV) All wrongdoing is sin

[20] John 3:17 (ESV) For all have sinned and fall short of the glory of God.

[21] Romans 8:1 (NKJV) There is therefore now no condemnation to those who are in Christ Jesus

(*thus affecting the amount of power we have given to what other people think of us*).

3. Because we are all sinners, we can then extend grace and encouragement to ourselves and others more freely. This builds relationship. Conversely, criticism, stemming from judgment, tears down relationships.

We may stop committing one sin, like murder, for example. However, the more we grow in our walk with God, the more we realize the plethora of other sins we commit.

One of the most powerful examples I have seen of this happened with a friend of mine. Her teenage son sexually abused another child in their neighborhood. The devastating news could have ripped their family to shreds. The family desperately needed love as they walked through the consequences of his actions with police, their neighbor, and others. Some people in their church body judged them. She told me that it was one of the hardest times in her life, but when a mutual friend of ours reminded her that "sin is sin" in God's eyes, she realized that those who condemned her and her son also were flagrantly sinning before God.

In times where love is desperately needed by those who hurt, flinging judgment only wounds more. My friend was able to *reject* condemnation and *receive* love from others. We need to be aware, also, that this tendency of Christians to "eat our own" via judgment instead of freely giving grace only increases the negative perceptions the world has of us. I have a friend whose daughter became pregnant at age seventeen. The daughter and her boyfriend were repentant and sorrowfully confessed to their parents, and then to their church body. Several months later, as my friend was leaving church, another friend asked how her daughter was doing. She shared about her daughter's upcoming wedding, the health of the baby growing inside her, and the job the baby's father had recently acquired. Her friend scowled. "What's wrong?" my friend asked.

"I don't think she suffered much for her sin," was her reply.

My friend was speechless for a moment. Then, as the Spirit moved her, she gently let her friend know how thankful they all were for what Jesus had done for them on the cross and how these sins had been removed as far away from them as the east is from the west. She asked her friend not to judge her daughter, as she was living in the freedom promised those of us who trust in Christ for our salvation. Both my friend and her daughter had found God's peace, comfort, and joy in the midst of difficulty, and that is a beautiful thing.

Instead of believing she had lost her position in the kingdom, my friend and her daughter saw their lives as abundant. Yes, teenage pregnancy and early marriage make life difficult and they are living through those difficulties. But, they are living through them with abundant blessing because they have accepted His gift and received forgiveness.

While the culture (secular or Christian) does a poor job of helping us develop a healthy understanding of who we are, who others are, and how we all fit together, it would be unwise to ignore the impact. Secular media reinforces all of the above notions of judgment and warped Christian teaching does the same. When we spend a majority of our time listening to secular song lyrics about sex and violence; exposing ourselves to images of seductive clothing either at the mall, online, or in magazines; or reading and/or watching fictional stories about characters with questionable morals (or worse yet, a majority of reality shows), our perception of what is holy begins to deteriorate. We have to make wise choices about the inputs into our mind, soul, and heart. If we put garbage in, we should not be surprised when we get garbage out. We'll find ourselves being catty, gossipy, covetous, or gluttonous rather quickly. Then we become self-focused and discover that those around us are not meeting our needs and God is no longer on the throne of our lives, Jesus is no longer Lord, and all we care about is the next thing that makes us happy. We stop our pursuit of God, and bind ourselves in worldly treasures, addictions, and false gods. We are no longer wise, but foolish.

One of my favorite passages in the Bible is about freedom:

To the Jews who had believed him, Jesus said, "If you hold to my teaching, you are really my disciples. Then you will know the truth, and the truth will set you free." *They answered him, "We are Abraham's descendants and have never been slaves of anyone. How can you say that we shall be set free?" Jesus replied, "I tell you the truth, everyone who sins is a slave to sin. Now a slave has no permanent place in the family, but a son belongs to it forever. So if the Son sets you free, you will be free indeed.* (John 8:31–36 NIV, emphasis mine)

Unknowingly becoming a slave to lies, I learned about marriage, motherhood, religion, and being a woman from what television, my parents, magazines, and my friends taught me as I grew up. Perhaps you learned some of these too.

Check off any you can relate to:

- ☐ Having a career is what matters most.
- ☐ Men are stupid.
- ☐ Women need to be thin, physically fit, long-haired, short-skirted, or use lots of make-up to be beautiful.
- ☐ Men are to be manipulated to get what you want.
- ☐ Women should be in charge of everyone at home.
- ☐ Women can easily be taken advantage of by men, and this is something to guard against.
- ☐ Men work all the time.
- ☐ Marriage is difficult, but if you marry the right guy, he will treat you like a princess and you will be happy.
- ☐ Men are lazy.
- ☐ Good marriages are full of romance.
- ☐ Bad marriages have conflict and are painful.
- ☐ Conflict is a bad thing.
- ☐ Sex is about power.
- ☐ Children are a pain and not necessary.
- ☐ Women are taken for granted by their families.
- ☐ Being a wife is an unfulfilling endeavor that makes women miserable.
- ☐ Being a good wife is about keeping a clean house, having the whitest whites, preparing gourmet meals every night, mothering, and lots of ironing.
- ☐ Children are to be seen and not heard.
- ☐ Children should be part of the adult conversations.
- ☐ If you are a good parent, your children behave perfectly.

☐ God is powerless.
☐ God/Religion is for weak people.
☐ Faith is for crazies.
☐ God does not exist.
☐ God no longer does miracles.
☐ Religion works for some people.
☐ If someone does something for you, it should be appreciated, regardless of what it is.
☐ If you do something for someone, they owe you.
☐ Approval from others matters greatly.
☐ Catching a man is one of the most important things for women.
☐ Respect is to be earned, but love should be unconditional.
☐ Having a great career is the most important thing for a woman.
☐ Being a mother is wonderful and fully rewarding.
☐ Being a mother is awful and exhausting.
☐ Husbands need constant correction.
☐ Husbands are always right and should never be corrected.
☐ Wives who confront their husband's sin are unsubmissive.
☐ Wives who fail to confront their husband's sin are more holy.
☐ Being submissive makes you a doormat.
☐ Being submissive is archaic.
☐ Respect is to be earned.
☐ Love is unconditional.
☐ Respect is unconditional.
☐ Love is conditional.
☐ Women are less important than men.
☐ Women are powerless.
☐ A woman needs a man to take care of her.

☐ A woman does not need anyone, especially a man, to take care of her.

☐ Women need to "stand up for their rights" or they will be taken advantage of by others.

☐ Women should look young, thin, and fashionable at any age (or they will not be able to catch and keep a man).

Other (add your own)*Take a look at the list, specifically the ones you have checked. Put a star next to the three that influenced you most.*

Think of the earliest moment in time when each of those lies was planted or deeply reinforced in your life. Describe each of them in your journal.

How About You?

1. *When you look at the amount of time each day that you spend watching television, listening to the radio, surfing online, looking at magazines, reading or listening to news, listening to podcasts, reading or listening to books, etc., what percentage of those would be considered secular?*

2. *When you look at the amount of time each day you spend with the Bible, in prayer, listening to God, worshiping Him, listening to Christian teachers via podcasts, television or radio, what percentage of your day is receiving godly input?*

3. *What do your percentages indicate about where your influences come from?*

4. *How have the lies you've believed and the media "inputs" you have allowed influenced your relationships with yourself, God, and others?*

5. *Ask God if these lies still deeply affect you. How so? Or have you found His victory? If so, how?*

   Knowing that all things work together for good for those who love God and are called according to His purpose[22], what good has come through these experiences—not the lies themselves, mind you, but how has God used these situations for good? (Dear God, please reveal Your Truth to us, in Jesus Christ's name, amen)

6. *Even though we believe lies, God is in the transformation business. It is likely that God has grown you and your marriage as a result of experiencing various hardships. Perhaps you are far enough on the other side of one of those hardships to see how God revealed His truth through the experience. What do you see now that you didn't before? And what will you do with what you learned?*

Chapter Dare:

Ask God to reveal how the culture has influenced you and to shine His light of Truth into your life. *Be open to the media influences around you, and choose more wisely what you allow contact with your eyes, ears, and heart. Do you really need to watch that sitcom? Does it honor men or women? Does it have values you want to pass along to*

---

[22] Romans 8:28

others? Why choose to be influenced by the lies of this world? The same applies to secular magazines, websites, music, movies, and the like. While we need to be "in the world" we also need to be careful to not be "of it." Bear in mind that if you do not stay up-to-date with some of secular culture, you also won't be someone of influence within it. Choose carefully how you will get information from the culture while guarding your heart. Because I am so easily swayed myself, I have to be very careful about what I watch on television or listen to on the radio. I strongly caution you to be extremely careful about what you choose to listen to, read, or watch, as much of it reinforces non-Biblical thinking and values.

Make Psalm 119:11 part of your daily time with God, hiding His Word in your heart that you might not sin against Him. If you are reading this book as part of the Daughters of Sarah® course, the "Steps of Faith" Scriptures are a great place to start.

Truth #7:

Satan is Real. He is the Father of Lies. His Goal is to Separate You and Others From God.

I remember standing in the aisle of the department store trying to pick out dish cloths for our kitchen. I had red ones in one hand and white ones in the other. I looked at my husband and said, "Honey, do you have an opinion about which of these you would like in the kitchen?" He gave me an eyebrow raise, and he said to me, "Nina, I married a woman that could make a decision. Where did she go?" I was in the middle of a ten year study on submission and respect in marriage. The current author of a book I was reading told us to ask our husbands his opinion about everything – to not make decisions without his input, otherwise we were trying to lead in the home.

In my efforts to be a good wife, I ran the gamut from beginning my journey as a dominating shrew to being a subservient doormat about halfway through. I was reading everything I could get my hands on – both secular and Christian – to learn how to be a good wife. I had a lot of influencers. I also confess that I drove my husband about half nuts while I was trying to figure out what God wanted me to do, working my way from rebelling against Him to discerning what obedience looked like. I did reach a point where I could discern what was true, however, and it was by focusing on reading the Bible. I finally figured out that God does not want me to be my husband's maid and cook, but rather his life partner, fully equal to him in our marriage. In our marriage, I also was responsible for certain aspects of the home management because I was there all day. Being his life partner means I have a voice in how we do marriage and family. It also means that my husband and I need to work together to do it well. We need each other.

I am still in the process of having His truth revealed to me and I feel certain this will be the case throughout the rest of my life. I do firmly believe, however, that God allowed extremely difficult circumstances (some as the result of my immature choices, others for reasons still not clear to me) in my life because He wanted me to be strong. He also wants me (and you) to rely on Him completely. *Those last two sentences might seem contradictory, but one does not exist without the other.*

We need to be aware of the spiritual war that rages around us. Sin entered the world through Satan and his tool is deception.

Be careful! Watch out for attacks from the Devil, your great enemy. He prowls around like a roaring lion, looking for some victim to devour. (1 Peter 5:8 NLT)

Satan has been deceiving human beings since we walked the earth. While we know that Christ is the conqueror, we also know that our foe is formidable and has a lot of experience with human behavior. He understands the nature of our flesh and uses that against us to entice us to believe the wrong things about ourselves, one another, and God. He wants us to exercise our own will, instead of obeying God, just like he does. Because he understands our sinful nature so well and because it is so similar to his own, he is very good at what he does.

He was a murderer from the beginning, and has nothing to do with the truth, because there is no truth in him. When he lies, he speaks out of his own character, for he is a liar and the father of lies. (John 8:44 ESV)

Many of the conflicts in relationships begin with misunderstandings and are based on lies. How often do we judge our husbands' motives? We assume that because they work long hours that they do not have any thoughts of us. However, research shows that their hard work to provide is one of the primary ways a man demonstrates love.[23] We assume when he speaks harshly, that he does not love us. We speak with emotion and he then thinks we are angry, when, in fact, we are hurting. We spend a ton of time in relationships criticizing and judging others instead of focusing on what good thing God is doing, or what is going right. We create an environment where lies are perpetuated and both people in the marriage are losing their contentment and sense of connection to the other. One of Satan's roles is that of "accuser" – we give too free of reign to him, don't we?

Satan's influence shows up in research by Gottman which demonstrates that a continual cycle of negative communication with a lack of positives will actually rewrite a couple's history together. This can even result in a history lacking in what was true or positive, with the

---

[23] Feldhahn, page 80

couple being able to only remember negative interpretations of events.[24]

We have to realize that many (if not most) of the negative perceptions we have about what other people think about us may be based on lies. Your perception of what your husband thinks or his perceptions of you might be inaccurate. We often are wrong when we believe we know what another person thinks. Realizing this can be tremendously freeing – if we will but communicate more to clarify what we think we are seeing or hearing, we will learn more about what is true.

We need to stop getting all of our exercise by jumping to conclusions!

Do you know what God thinks of you? When asked, most people respond with something negative, but that simply is not true. If you do not believe God thinks you are awesome, you do not fully understand what He did for you with Jesus Christ. If you were the only person on the planet, He still would have sent Jesus to die and pay the penalty for your sins. Refusing to believe you are precious and important to God is like refusing Christ.

Do not feel guilty for not understanding this, however. It takes most people a while to grasp the concept of God's great love for us – and most of us struggle with believing it off and on during our Christian journey. Lies are all around us, both in and out of the church that make this hard.

What I personally found most difficult to reconcile was the incongruity between my marital happiness and my faith. I

---

[24] Gottman, page 42

had bought into one of the lies some in the Christian culture promulgate. Perhaps you are familiar with it: the lie that if we follow Jesus, we will not have any more suffering or troubles. I remember hearing one woman say to a group of younger women that if we were not happy in our marriages, we just did not have enough faith. If we weren't happy, we were not praying, obeying, or serving enough. I did not know enough about following Jesus to feel anything but frustrated.

So I worked harder at my faith and being a better wife. I signed up to serve everywhere I could. I even pretended I was happy because I thought I was not a good enough Christian if I was not smiling all the time. I worked part-time and tried very hard to be excellent as an employee. Most people in my personal life were Christians, and they certainly seemed happy. What I did not realize was that some legitimately were filled with joy and others were merely pretending, as I was. I could not tell the difference.

Hopefully you have been smarter than me and have not gone down this path of pretending. If you have, however, you know it leads to discouragement. Perhaps the most important thing I did not realize at this time was that I was simply an immature follower of Christ. I did not know very much about the Bible, God's character, or how I could have a personal relationship with Him—or what that even actually looked like.

The most damaging part of this immaturity revealed itself when I became painfully aware of how much I wanted to be encouraged by and affirmed by the man I married. I did not make time for any of my own interests nor was I filled with the Holy Spirit and, as a result, for nearly the first full decade of our marriage, I looked to my husband to fill too many of my emotional needs. I had created an idol in my marriage, a fulfillment of Genesis 3:16, "Yet your desire will be for your husband." Whether that verse deals with our desire for control or our actual turning to our husbands instead of God (in terms of fulfilling our emotional and relational needs), is irrelevant; the outcome emerges the same: disappointment.

Over the centuries, some attention has been given to the word commonly translated as *desire*, from Genesis 3:16. For around five hundred years, the word in the text translated as *turning*, which means "an emotional yearning in a certain direction." *Our desire should be for our God,* for Jesus, for the Lover of our souls, but, instead, it is for our husbands. Because of Eve's deception, however, women long for relationship and fulfillment from their husbands instead of God.

I also have heard this passage taught frequently as "The Curse of Eve," however, nothing in the original text specifically mentions the word *curse* in relation to her. Yes, there are consequences for her because of what has happened, but she readily admits that she was deceived and she blames the serpent. The ground is cursed for the man, and the serpent itself is cursed. The serpent tricked Eve, and she added to God's words, saying they would die if they ate from the tree. It is interesting that in two other places the Bible mentions how we should not add to God's words or we will be rebuked, proven a liar, and receive plagues.[25] It is interesting that John refers to Satan as a "murderer from the start" (John 8:44). That cunning serpent orchestrated the death of innocence, ushering in pain and hardship for us all.

---

[25] Proverbs 30:5-6, Revelation 22:18

The text also says that Adam was with Eve. Adam's passivity is actually the first sin, and Eve's adding to what God said, the second. Thinking about the great weight and responsibility of communicating God's Word to others makes me shudder with reverence and caution. I wonder about those of us who attempt to encourage others to obey God's Word by discussing it with others. I am ever more thankful for Christ's sacrifice and payment for our sins as I doubt that any of us fully understand all of the Bible well enough to teach it without committing sin, myself included. It concerns me that many of the teachings I have received seem to swing either too conservatively or too liberally in the discussion of Eve and her effect on women's roles today.

Maybe you can relate to where I have been. I want to take a moment to encourage you. As I grew closer to God, my need for affirmation from people diminished. My desire for accolades from my husband disappeared completely. God not only met my need for affirmation through relationship with Him, He helped me grow my strengths through relationships with many others, including my husband. I learned I needed to spend intentional time each week filling myself with encouragement from people who built me up and solid Christian teaching. I learned the value of a Sabbath and started taking intentional rest without guilt. I am praying you also find this freedom and rest that He offers all of us!

I know very few women who are so connected to God that they are comfortable in their own skins. I am bothered by teachers who portray all wives as "shadows" of their husbands and emphasize only one mold for us as women. This mold always looks similar, with only a few variations:

a woman deeply fulfilled by washing dishes, doing laundry, preparing gourmet meals, sewing every torn piece of clothing, keeping the tidiest of homes, ironing lavender-scented sheets, all while focusing only on the achievements of her husband and children.

Please do not misunderstand, I believe strongly that wives should care for their homes and families, but I also know that living life vicariously through others is very dangerous. Having said that, I have a number of friends who *really do find fulfillment in being homemakers*—and I do not fault them for that. They are doing what God has called them to do and I admire them for it. They love it and I love that they love it! I homeschool my own children and treasure my time with them. I am thankful for my family and our intimate relationships, and yet still have worked part-time since having children. But because I am disabled, I cannot sew or maintain a spotless home, even with help. I peeled and canned just two bushels of pears one summer with a friend and was in pain and unable to do much for nearly two weeks as a result.

To hold myself to the perfect homemaker status simply makes me feel like a failure because it is physically impossible for me to measure up. Am I less of a woman or a failure as a Christian wife because I cannot physically do as much? There are many other women who make themselves better moms because they invest in a God-given love of horses, biking, scrap booking, or other hobbies, or even part-time employment situations that are passions for them. God made every one of us with unique passions and talents. To deny the existence of those things within us is to deny Creation itself, in my opinion. Scripture also speaks to this in 1 Peter 4:10–11: As each has received a gift, use it to serve one another, as good stewards of God's varied grace: whoever speaks, as one who speaks oracles of God; whoever serves, as one who serves by the strength that God supplies—in order that in everything God may be glorified through Jesus Christ. To him belong glory and dominion forever and ever. Amen.

The other extremist side of the coin is just as destructive. We have to be careful not to focus only on the Bible texts that talk about friendship and "mutual submission" while avoiding, love, respect, submit, and the hierarchy of the family. God ordained the family structure as communicated in Genesis 2 and 3. A lack of attention to the whole picture also may fuel the divorce statistics within the church. In my limited experience, few devout Christians—including therapists, psychologists, counselors and pastors—seem to be really talented at conflict resolution. It is true, however, that when men are more loving in conflict and women are more respectful, things tend to go better.

Encouraging us to "fight for our rights" flies in the face of Christ's teaching. Being a woman of strength and dignity does not mean marriage is only about friendship and the domestic chores distribution set at fifty–fifty.

Denying the hierarchy established by God in families also is dangerous. Mutual submission is not a beginning place for most but rather a destination where respect, love, and an attitude of servant-hood for those involved abound. Both women and men need to recognize that what is true for Christ is true for all—the least of us will be greatest.

> An argument arose among them as to which of them was the greatest. But Jesus, knowing the reasoning of their hearts, took a child and put him

by his side and said to them, "Whoever receives this child in my name receives me, and whoever receives me receives him who sent me. *For he who is least among you all is the one who is great.*" (Luke 9:46–48 ESV, emphasis added)

When he had washed their feet and put on his outer garments and resumed his place, he said to them, "Do you understand what I have done to you? You call me Teacher and Lord, and you are right, for so I am. *If I then, your Lord and Teacher, have washed your feet, you also ought to wash one another's feet. For I have given you an example, that you also should do just as I have done to you.* Truly, truly, I say to you, a servant is not greater than his master, nor is a messenger greater than the one who sent him. If you know these things, blessed are you if you do them." (John 13:12–17 ESV, emphasis added)

Jesus crossed many different cultural boundaries by loving and including children, by seeking out people of different ethnicity, and by including women in His teachings and His ministries. He turned the culture of His time upside down, and was the absolute best thing to ever happen to women. At a time when other men and church leaders told men not to bother teaching women, Jesus Christ made it a point to teach women. When Martha complained that her sister Mary was not helping her prepare for all the guests, Jesus told her Mary had chosen the better thing by sitting at His feet and learning.

As Jesus and his disciples were on their way, he came to a village where a woman named Martha opened her home to him. She had a sister called

Mary, who sat at the Lord's feet listening to what he said. But Martha was distracted by all the preparations that had to be made. She came to him and asked, "Lord, don't you care that my sister has left me to do the work by myself? Tell her to help me!"

"Martha, Martha," the Lord answered, "you are worried and upset about many things, *but few things are needed—or indeed only one. Mary has chosen what is better, and it will not be taken away from her.*" (Luke 10:38–42 NIV, emphasis added)

I also see Jesus saying to Martha, "We can figure out the food and everything else when we need to. There is only one thing that matters here, and Mary is doing it. You need to just chill." Please forgive my "Bible according to Nina" loose translation, but I really believe He wants something other than what we try to offer. He wants time with us.

Today in our culture we shy away from having people in our homes because of clutter, spent light bulbs, and the need for cleaning, painting, whatever. None of that matters. Do you see what Christ is saying? We matter more than the state of our homes to Him. Relationship is more important to Him than what is for dinner. If you have overscheduled yourself or your children, know you are choosing matters of lesser importance over the Most Important One.

Realize, as well, that women are equal heirs in the kingdom of God.[26] Yes, we are smaller in stature and

---

[26] 1 Peter 3:7 (ESV) Likewise, husbands, live with your wives in an understanding way, showing honor to the woman as the weaker

physically not as strong, but God views women as equal
heirs and as made in God's own image.

> Then God said, "Let Us make man in Our Image,
> according to Our likeness; *let them have dominion*
> *over* the fish of the sea, over the birds of the air,
> and over the cattle, over all the earth and over
> every creeping thing that creeps on the earth." *So*
> *God created man in His own image; in the image of*
> *God He created him; male and female He created*
> *them.* (Genesis 1:26–27 ESV, emphasis added)

God created men and women in His own image and as
equal heirs to grace. While a woman's role is not
minimized, *it has a few behaviors defined within marriage*
just *as a man's does*. Many men might relish trading the
stress that comes with the "thistles," "painful toil," and
"sweat," of his work to the burden or stress that comes
with being under someone else's protection. Perhaps they
would not want to trade, but the point is that they have
their consequence and we have ours. Who are we to argue
with God? Bible commentator Matthew Henry said that
Eve was *"made of a rib out of the side of Adam; not made*
out of his head to rule over him, nor out of his feet to be
trampled upon by him, but out of his side to be equal with
him, under his arm to be protected, and near his heart to
be beloved."[27]

I only am sharing with you what is clearly in the Bible. God
wants us to figure out the details for ourselves and our
marriages in a way that brings glory to Him. I do think,

---

vessel, since they are heirs with you of the grace of life, so that your
prayers may not be hindered.

[27] Henry, Matthew, A Commentary on the Whole Bible, vol. 1, Fleming
Revell Company, Old Tappan, New Jersey, p. 20, n.d.

however, it is wrong to cast judgment on another woman for how she and her husband "do marriage." We need to give one another the freedom to be how He created us, instead of worshiping some ideal—Christian, secular, or otherwise—in the hope it will bring us happiness. Our fulfillment of our purpose should be found in our relationship with Christ.

This misplacement of our desire in the form of a perfect ideal is a form of idolatry, which even though we are lacking in awareness of this sin, is still a sin. It also negatively affects our relationships with ourselves, our husbands, and our God. We miss an opportunity when we put our hope in anything but Christ. Sometimes the opportunities are huge:

> Likewise, wives, be subject to your own husbands, so that *even if some do not obey the word, they may be won without a word by the conduct of their wives,* when they see your respectful and pure conduct. Do not let your adorning be external—the braiding of hair and the putting on of gold jewelry, or the clothing you wear—but let your adorning be the hidden person of the heart with the imperishable beauty of a gentle and quiet spirit, which in God's sight is very precious. For this is how the holy women *who hoped in God* used to adorn themselves, by submitting to their own husbands, as Sarah obeyed Abraham, calling him lord. And you are her children, if you do good and do not fear anything that is frightening. Likewise, husbands, live with your wives in an understanding way, *showing honor to the woman as the weaker vessel, since they are heirs with you of the grace of life, so*

that your prayers may not be hindered. (1 Peter 3:1–7 ESV, emphasis added)

I added the emphasis to point out that even our husbands who do not know the Lord can be saved by seeing Christ in us. There are obviously huge dividends, opportunities, and consequences to putting our hope in Christ. Doing so means we are His—and with this comes great comfort and great sacrifice at the same time.

The women from long ago put their hope in God, and we are (and have been, through the ages) equal heirs in God's kingdom. We are not "less than" men, but different. Why we view our physically smaller, less muscle massed selves as "less than" is lunacy. So what if women are smaller and physically weaker than men? Most cats are smaller than and not as strong as dogs—that likely seldom makes them think they should aspire to be dogs! If you are familiar with cats, you can probably agree that they tend to think very highly of themselves!

Did you notice verse 7 in the 1 Peter passage? God told men to keep our differences in mind. *God feels so strongly and tenderly toward women that He basically tells men their prayers will not be heard if they do not treat their wives with honor.*

One of the problems we run into when buying the lie of seeing ourselves as "less than" is inadvertently creating oppressors out of those around us—regardless of what is actually true. I know there are oppressive men out there. What I am speaking to now, however, is the average guy, who is just trying to do life with the girl he married. Personally, early in our marriage, I wasted too much time causing conflict over minutia in an effort to "stand up for my rights," with a man who would willingly protect my rights if I had given him the chance.

I did not realize my wrong thinking at the time and would have been shocked had someone suggested my pursuits and hopes were actually idolatry in action. My dream and reality collided in one painful and memorable moment in time. My boss called me into his office and began discussing my recent decline in productivity. Married for barely a year, the reality of sharing close quarters with another human had set in. That "twitter-pated" feeling where one is deliriously distracted and nearly unable to breathe properly at the thought of the other . . . well, it also had vanished.

In my immaturity, I was unaware and unprepared for this next phase of love[28] and grew extremely disappointed. Having bought the lies of the culture, the rush of hormone-induced euphoria of infatuation had addicted me to love—and it had vanished. I had no idea this was actually normal for most people. As my superior looked at me and asked what was going on, I responded by bursting into tears, momentarily throwing professionalism out the window.

Then I was crying *because I was crying*, shocked at the depth of my reaction. I blubbered, "I think I married the wrong person!" and proceeded to whine about how I no longer felt in love, and I had no idea what to do.

Reacting like most men when faced with a sobbing woman, he did not know what to do, either. He did

---

[28] Most experts tell us there are three stages of love: 1) Infatuation, 2) Conflict, and 3) Harvest.

manage to hand me a tissue, tell me to chin up and work harder or something motivational, then stood up to encourage me to get out of his office. To both our relief, I promptly left.

While I would have liked to tell you that early in my marriage I had this whole area figured out, that is obviously not true. What I have discovered and heard repeatedly from other women around the country, is this:

> *The deeper my relationship with my God,*
> *the better my marriage is.*

When I wander away from our Lord or fail to take time once a week to do things that fill and energize me, which happens sometimes, I immediately start turning toward my husband for affirmation and encouragement. It is often during those times that my husband and I begin to struggle again in our marriage. Unfortunately, our husbands cannot satisfy those God-sized places in our hearts; we need something supernatural. Humankind has spent centuries attempting to replace relationship with God with other humans, things, and habits. It simply is not possible.

Comfort dwells in my soul when I remember that, like Israel, God's children are in a constant state of turning and returning. The Bible is populated with multiple stories painting the picture of God's pursuit. When the tribe of Israel turns away from God, He pursues her. Consider Hosea 6 (ESV) where not only do we find a husband pursuing his philandering wife, but our God pursuing His people.

Come, let us return to the LORD. For He has torn us, but He will heal us; He has wounded us, but He will bandage us. He will revive us after two days; He will raise us up on the third day, that we may live before Him. So let us know, let us press on to know the LORD. His going forth is as certain as the dawn; and He will come to us like the rain, like the spring rain watering the earth.

What shall I do with you, O Ephraim? What shall I do with you, O Judah? For your loyalty is like a morning cloud and like the dew which goes away early. Therefore I have hewn them in pieces by the prophets; I have slain them by the words of My mouth; and the judgments on you are like the light that goes forth. For I delight in loyalty rather than sacrifice, and in the knowledge of God rather than burnt offerings. *But like Adam they have transgressed the covenant; there they have dealt treacherously against Me.*

Gilead is a city of wrongdoers, tracked with bloody footprints. And as raiders wait for a man, so a band of priests murder on the way to Shechem; surely they have committed crime. In the house of Israel I have seen a horrible thing; Ephraim's harlotry is there, Israel has defiled itself. Also, *O Judah, there is a harvest appointed for you, when I restore the fortunes of My people.*

In raising my children, I try hard to focus on helping them understand their identity in Christ. Knowing who He is and what He did matters first, then understanding who I am now as a result of my beliefs and relationship with God makes all the difference in the world. We then can live this life for the Audience of One—whose opinion is truly the only one that matters. We must continually come back to this Truth, otherwise we are easily deceived by the enemy. I can do this better, but never perfectly, in my marriage when I keep my own identity wrapped up in Christ's perception of me.

How about you?

1. *Before your wedding day, what dreams did you have for your marriage? How have they changed?*

2. *Where are you now? How would you describe the state of your marriage?*

3. *Have you found yourself being useful to Satan as the "accuser" in your relationships? Do you build up or tear down those around you?*

4. *What other desires have interfered with your desire for God?*

5. *Has your desire been more for your husband instead of God?*

6. *How has this desire affected you or your relationships, including your relationship with God?*

7. *What times have you had when your relationship with God took care of every need? If you are not there now, who or what is competing with God to take care of your needs? What steps do you need to take to return?*

Chapter Dares:

Dare 1: Prayerfully confess any misplaced desires to our Lord. Ask Him for help in setting your desires and hopes in Him and His Son, Jesus Christ. Consider who you might invite to help you become accountable in this area.

Trust and know He forgives you completely. If you have trouble doing this, ask Him for help. Remember 1 John 1:9: "If we confess our sins, he is faithful and righteous to forgive us our sins, and to cleanse us from all unrighteousness."

Dare 2: Add the practice of silence to your communication repertoire—and do not take offense at the suggestion. *We will discuss this in detail in upcoming chapters. Stop letting Satan use you as his instrument as the "accuser." Catch your tongue before it lets unwholesome talk come out of your mouth[29] and instead only speak that which is edifying toward others.[30] Stop the communication behaviors that, if pervasive, have the power to destroy your marriage. Gottman calls the following the "Four Horsemen of the Apocalypse":*

- Criticism *(pointing out another's mistakes or flaws)*
- Contempt *(disrespect, disgust, etc., usually via tone and facial expressions—eye rolling, sarcasm, pursed lips, scowling, etc.)*
- Defensiveness *(often shows up as frequent disagreement with others, keeping a list of wrongs*

---

[29] Proverbs 10:19 (NIV) When Words are many, sin is not absent, but he who holds his tongue is wise.

[30] Ephesians 4:29 (NIV) Do not let any unwholesome talk come out of your mouths, but only what is helpful for building others up according to their needs, that it may benefit those who listen.

so that when asked a question you feel attacked
and respond by defending yourself)

- Stonewalling *(refusing to engage in communication*
  verbally or nonverbally with your husband when he
  wants to talk—many men do this, but women also
  do this when they have given up on the
  relationship).

Truth #8:

Submission Has a Bad Rap but is a Good Thing.

Early in our marriage, Jim and I joined a small group to study the Bible. One night, about two years into our journey as a couple and during the small group's study on marriage, we had to rate our marriage as part of an activity. I kept telling everyone I did not want to participate. They pressed. Finally, I acquiesced. I gave us a two out of ten with ten being great. My husband nearly fell out of his chair. Mouths open, our friends stared. By this time, we had attended a number of marriage conferences, read several books together, taken marriage classes, and studied marriage with our small group. Everyone in the room was surprised, including Jim.

Obviously, I was miserable, and still did not know why. My head was filled with "if only" thoughts: *if only* Jim worked fewer hours; *if only* he bought me flowers; *if only* he said nice things to me; *if only* he asked me questions; *if only* he listened more; *if only* he told me I was pretty; *if only* he were more like so-and-so on television or so-and-so's husband; *if only* he commented on the positives; *if only* he appreciated my efforts to maintain my body and looks for him. I constantly focused on the negatives. Completely blinded by selfishness, I judged my husband. I did not even know these thoughts were sinful. I had a "plank in my own eye"[31] and was blinded by it.

I also was seriously busy judging myself. The "if only" thoughts directed at myself went something like, *If only I were thinner; if only I were a better cook; if only I had better hair; if only I were more adventurous; if only I always had the laundry done; if only I was more like his mother; if only I were better at managing money; if only I were smarter; if only I could be more fit; if only I was prettier; if only . . .* I thought if I were somehow "better" that Jim would demonstrate his love to me once again.

In addition to the plank of judgment in one eye looking at my husband, my other eye was blinded by judgment toward myself. This is condemnation, an unhealthy perception of self and others, that originates in pride or desiring the praise and approval of other people. It is sin.

These sinful thoughts resulted in my having a weak relationship with God. I was immature and did not even know it. Since I was seeing other Christian marriages that seemed genuinely fulfilling for both people, I was even more frustrated because we did not seem to be figuring things out.

I spent nearly six years trying to learn why I was so disappointed with my marriage, all the while still growing in my faith. I was really just filling my head with Biblical knowledge, which is a necessary part of growth. However, the relationship aspect of faith and the joy and peace elements were completely missing. There were times when I was angry at my husband and, like many women,

---

[31] Matthew 7:3 (ESV) Why do you see the speck that is in your brother's eye, but do not notice the log that is in your own eye?

sometimes even afraid of my husband when he was angry. Mostly I just yearned for deeper connection with him and the friendship we enjoyed so much in our early days. I was working on outward appearances—both my own, my husband's, and the appearance our marriage presented. My judgment emerged as criticism. Being a bit of a perfectionist, I was quick to criticize. My husband, also a perfectionist, responded in kind.

As I grew in my knowledge of the Bible, I began to have mixed feelings. I wavered between being angry at God for telling me to respect and submit to a man who I felt did not love me. I was wrong to assume he did not love me, but it was what I believed. I began to judge my husband even more, based on what I was learning from the Christian studies on marriage we were doing in our small group. The "if only's" idol morphed into, *If only* he were more of a spiritual leader like Dr. James Dobson; *if only* he were as patient as Gary Smalley.

I started adjusting my expectations to include those within the Christian culture. Perhaps the biggest mistake I made during this time was being blind to the way God had created my husband. Instead of focusing on his strengths, I could only see the negatives. This clouded my vision such that I began to perceive even neutral behaviors or events as negative.

If he came home from work late, I thought it was because he did not want to see me. If he forgot to do something I asked him to do, I thought I was not important to him. If he took care of himself by spending time with a friend, I thought he did not want to spend time with me. I did not ask him whether my perceptions were accurate; I simply harbored bad feelings and resentment and became useful to the enemy as the weeks progressed.

Firmly convinced that spiritual leadership specifically looked like an episode from one of the Christian radio programs we listened to regularly, my judgment deepened further. Certain that Christian folk spent their evenings with a dear husband reading a verse from Proverbs as the entire family gathered around the dinner table, I placed even higher expectations on my husband. As God was barely beginning to untangle my secular beliefs based on lies, I felt confident that the Christian culture had it right.

I am not discounting or criticizing how some families live out their faith. I appreciate the examples from Christian radio and various authors for those of us who did not grow up in homes where Christ or referencing the Bible for daily advice and guidance was a focus. What I completely missed, however, was the grace-love-forgiveness of God's heart. I completely missed the Biblical message of "Trust God, and you will find peace and joy."

Somehow I also missed the message that knowing Him changes your heart. The goal is to spend forever getting to know Him so you can become like Him from the inside out—in that order. I spent my time trying to "look" like a Christian, instead of simply being one. I tried very hard to "do" Christianity, to "do" faith, instead of asking Him to transform me into His image. I needed to simply follow Him and surrender my life to Him. I desperately needed to know Him, not just know about Him. I needed transformation, Romans 12:1–2 (KJV) style:

> I beseech you therefore, brethren, by the mercies of God, to present your bodies a living sacrifice,

holy, acceptable to God, which is your spiritual
service. And be not fashioned according to this
world: but be ye transformed by the renewing of
your mind, and ye may prove what is the good and
acceptable and perfect will of God.

The secular culture communicates confusing and
contradictory concepts to women, often resulting in eating
disorders, unreasonable expectations for marriage, and
frustration as we attempt to gain our sense of value from
people around us, from the mirror, and from the
bathroom scale. What we should be reinforcing to
ourselves and teaching our daughters is the worth that is
within us simply because we are God's creations and He
loves us. *This understanding of where our worth comes
from helps us desire only God to define our worth and
identity, instead of our husband.*

Another concept that frightens us and hinders our growth
experience and relationship with God is "submission" and
"surrender."

Think about the words *submit* and *surrender* for a
moment. Chew on them.

*What emotions begin to attach themselves to these
words?*

I have seen numerous Christian and a few secular
teachings on the word *submit* as it pertains to a woman in
a marriage. Before discussing those, however, let's address
how *submit* fits into our relationship with God. *How we
view the concept of submitting to God's authority (by
obeying His Word) shapes our experience of relationships.*
If we view the Bible as a book of good ideas or

suggestions, we leave ourselves a lot of room to make decisions outside His will, which is disobedience.

We also need to remember that we regularly submit to authority every day – and are supposed to. This creates order. Imagine what would happen if we all (or even one of us) decided to stop submitting to the authority of our government and ceased obeying traffic lights. If I work, I submit to the rules of my employer and follow my boss's direction. When I worked in corporate training, we often would have classes with several trainers. Who was in charge of the class varied from class to class. Sometimes I was the lead trainer, sometimes it was someone else. We respectfully deferred the final say to the person who was held accountable for the class. Never once did we consider ourselves as "less than" someone else. We need to look at marriage the same way. Our husband is held accountable and is responsible for our family.

Another important truth in discussing submission is how God views us and how we perceive Him. If we see Him as angry or aloof, instead of as a loving Father who deeply cherishes us and wants to interact with us daily, we will not view submission or surrender in a positive light. If we ascribe our negative experiences with our earthly fathers or other men to Him, we also are not seeing the truth clearly.

We need to open our hearts up to His truth of who we are because we are His. We can then more easily see the Bible as a living document through which God Himself speaks into our daily lives with helpful instruction.

> *Let us therefore give diligence to enter into that rest, that no man fall after the same example of*

disobedience. For the word of God is living, and active, and sharper than any two-edged sword, and piercing even to the dividing of soul and spirit, of both joints and marrow, and quick to discern the thoughts and intents of the heart. And there is no creature that is not manifest in His sight: but all things are naked and laid open before the eyes of Him with whom we have to do.

Having then a great high priest, who hath passed through the heavens, Jesus the Son of God, let us hold fast our confession. For we have not a high priest that cannot be touched with the feeling of our infirmities; but one that hath been in all points tempted like as we are, yet, without sin. Let us therefore draw near with boldness unto the throne of grace, that we may receive mercy, and may find grace to help us in time of need. (Hebrews 4:11–16 KJV)

Trusting God as the perfect Father means we understand we have someone in charge who is more knowledgeable than us; stronger than us; deeply motivated to protect, grow, and nurture us; *and therefore we are safe.* This trust is the element through which a deep relationship in God can be formed. *When we trust, we can more easily submit—and we will even want to submit.*

One of the best descriptions of who we are in Christ came from a woman who wrote the following in the comment section of my blog:

I think our correct understanding of who we are in Christ is critical to understanding our role in all of our relationships, including marriage. How do I relate to others? I need only look to Christ for my example. Ideally, my husband is doing the same. Regardless of that, (my husband's actions), I can still look to Christ, cling to Him, and be renewed in my mind and have my heart attitudes and actions conformed to the living Word. I can trust Him because there is nothing He cannot do and nothing that can separate me from His love. (Romans 8:38–39; Job 26; Psalm 62; Isaiah 40:28–30; Ephesians 3:14–20).

Nowhere does the Bible say woman is less than, inferior, or sub-par to that of man. Quite on the contrary, Christ was sent by the Father to lay down His life for all human life – sinful man and sinful woman.

Does God like women? Just look at Jesus and His interactions with women. It is breathtaking and beautiful. In a society and Jewish culture that gave woman no status, rights, or freedoms, where Jewish law subjugated women and reduced them to a possession to be discarded at a man's will, Jesus went to the woman at the well, spoke to her heart, and met her need for living water (John 4:7–42). Jesus turned around and looked at the woman washing his feet with her tears, and he praised her. He used her to teach the Pharisee Simon about love and laid bare the arrogance and pride that prevented it, and then He forgave her sin and gave her peace (Luke 7:36–50). When He saw a crippled woman, bent over for eighteen years, He called her to Him! He immediately healed her. He gave a woman with no hope a new life that glorified God. In many ways her bent-over body represented what the women of that time must have felt like—no hope, defeated, helpless. Jesus again used a woman to point out the hypocrisy and shame in the Pharisees' attitudes and behavior, while at the same time giving hope to all those in bondage (Luke 13:10–17).

The woman, caught in adultery and brought to Jesus in humiliation, found mercy instead of condemnation. Sin, shame, and hypocrisy rested not on the adulterous woman, but upon the men who tried to use her in hopes of trapping Jesus (John 8:1–11). God chose a woman to carry and give birth to the Savior. What a beautiful portrait of courage and humility we have in Mary of Nazareth (Luke 1:26–56). There have been many women God has commissioned in His work, and He named them in His holy Word so that we would know it. Abigail, Anna, Rebecca, Rachel, Mary Magdalene, Mary and Martha, Sarah, Deborah, Dorcas/ Tabitha, Esther, Hannah, Lydia, Ruth and Naomi, Huldah, Eve, Elizabeth, Jael, Priscilla, Phoebe—to name some. Many have said, rightly so, that Christianity—Jesus—is the liberator of women. Truly, Jesus is the emancipator of us all.

To be clear, I do not think I am superior to my husband, nor am I inferior. I see us as equal, obviously different, but equally loved by God, both sinners saved by grace through faith in Christ. We are joint heirs with Christ; we are both children of Abraham by faith; and we are both of equal value and worth to God. There is "no partiality with God" (Rom. 2:10–12; Eph. 6:8–9; Acts 10:34–35).
~Angie

Remember, God's ways are not our ways and frequently God's ways fly in the face of conventional secular wisdom. We are weak when we are strong; we are raised high when we humbly lower ourselves. Our flesh will not like the concept of submission, but we must lay this down, not struggle against it, and *ask God to teach us* how to submit. Nothing I (or anyone else) tell you can teach you this—this is something only God can teach you.

My struggle with submission ended when I realized that God's plan for marriage had nothing to do with God's view of women. Clearly, He would not encourage women to teach other women or raise their children if we were not worthy of influencing others. He would have told us to keep quiet 100 percent of the time; yet, when we examine the Bible, we see women who are prophets and others involved in ministry activities. I learned to see submission as:

1) simply being kind and gentle in the way I communicated, not being argumentative when I disagreed – in other words, not being a disagreeable person; and

2) accepting the fact that God held my husband accountable for the outcome of our marriage and family – he was CEO, but I was the President, and he needed my help and input.

We all are familiar with families completely run by the wives—some of us even grew up in them. In many of these homes, it's common also to see extremely passive husbands. I do not know about you, maybe you want a passive husband? I, however, do not. Women are fully capable of leading (what mother is not a leader?) and have so many strengths in relationships. I believe God wants women to use this gifting carefully to avoid arousing conflict with our husbands, making things easier for them and easier for our families to function.

A man who is argumentative and immature or has severe trust or control issues will be more difficult to live with and will create many circumstances in which his wife will need to submit. This is but one of the reasons it is important to choose a husband wisely. I believe, however, that our husbands are told to love us to make it easier for us to respect them and because love fills up most women. We are told to respect our husbands because, as women, we are naturally gifted at being loving, but struggle with showing respect.

I also have seen God wait for our obedience before answering our prayers. Many women who have tried to manipulate their husbands into demonstrating love for them have failed miserably. Decades ago, I was one of them, but God has healed me of that deceptive behavior and misplaced yearning. We have seen many wives receive this highly sought after love only after learning how to consistently respect their husbands. And, for what it is worth, we should be respectful of all people, not just our husbands. Unfortunately, many women struggle with being respectful, not just in the home, but in all areas of their lives.

Because deeper relationship with God is born out of obedience to God, perhaps in some situations we need to submit to God by submitting to and respecting our husbands as God commands. My point is that God created families as an organization with marriage at the heart, and each marriage is going to look a little different—and that is okay. *We have to figure these differences out within the contexts of our own marriages. Being respectful, however, is always the way we should treat other people, whether we are married to them or not.*

I remember reading years ago that a wife was never to correct her husband's driving, but rather to allow him to take the wrong turn, be late, whatever, *but not to let him know he is making a mistake.* When I asked my own husband what he thought about this method, he basically told me that if I were to allow him to miss an exit and be late, fully knowing he was doing the wrong thing, I was not being a very good friend to him. He added that if I gave him the information in a way that made him appear stupid that would be disrespectful, and he would not appreciate this kind of treatment. Too many of our sentences have a "you idiot!" tone to them. There is a dramatic difference between saying, "Honey, I think that's our exit right there" and "I can't believe you are going to miss our exit—you never pay attention to how you drive!"

While the author of what I read may have had a husband who would have been offended by her help, mine would not—the opposite would have been true. This is why we stress communication as key in all relationships. Yes, we are to sacrifice for and love our husbands and our children well, but they are to love us too. Such is the life of a Christ-follower, submitting to God's teachings of love and respect in the Bible, regardless of gender.

How about you?

1. *What are some of the "if only's" you have adopted for your husband? Yourself? Your marriage?*

2. *Have your perceptions become negative? What neutral behaviors or events have become clouded by negative perceptions?*

3. *Have you struggled in the area of appearances, either Christian or secular? How much energy have you put into trying to "look" a certain way?*

4. *How does the idea of surrendering your whole life to God strike you? Does it scare you or empower you?*

5. *What negative ideas has the world communicated to us with regard to the word submission? When you think of submission, what images come to mind for you?*

6. *What about the word* surrender?

7. *Perhaps your ability or inability to submit is rooted in what you believe about God Himself and how He sees you. What is true for you in this regard right now? How much trust do you have in God? Have you misplaced that trust by placing it onto other people?*

8. *How practiced are you at submitting to God's authority? What areas are still under your control? What, if anything, needs to change for you in this area?*

9. *How does the practice of submission to God's authority influence your submission to your husband's leadership in your marriage?*

10. *Confess the truth of where you are and how you see yourself to God, and either respond with thanksgiving for what He has taught you, or ask Him to help you create a new, healthier, more accurate understanding of Him so your trust in Him can grow.*

Chapter Dares:

Dare 1: Continue the practices of "silence," apologizing and forgiving in your communication repertoire— without taking offense at the suggestion. Encourage others with what you say to them, focusing on the positives and not the negatives. Get rid of criticism, contempt, defensiveness, and stonewalling.

Dare 2: Create opportunities to intentionally submit to your husband. This will give you practice in submission and your husband practice in leading. Ask your husband for his opinion about a small decision, do what he suggests, thanking him for his input. Be careful not to start with something too small or it might frustrate him! Increase the size or importance of the decisions, until you are involving him in the most important aspects of your lives. If you live with a disagreeable or critical man, it is wise to start out your conversations with, "This might be a silly idea, but I wondering if you think I should do A or B," or "I'm really struggling with what to do and would like your advice on whether I should do A or B." If you have a desire to take action on one option over another, present the one you prefer second, unless he typically rejects the last option he hears. Many critical people often reject the first option presented to them.

As you read through these dares, which pose a challenge to you? How will you meet that challenge? What do you need God's help with? Write out your prayer requests in your journal.:

Truth #9:

Choosing Submission Does Not Make You a Doormat but It Does Take a Ton of Trust in God.

We often travel back to the Rocky Mountains for family vacations. Whitewater rafting often captures our attention, and sometimes we go. Instead of renting kayaks or a boat and venturing out on our own on a turbulent stretch of the river, however, we pay a guide service and join a group of other rafters so we can experience these thrills in a safer way.

In the middle of each boat of about six to ten rafters, an experienced guide sits on a perch, with two long oars, one extending to each side of the boat. He hands us a life jacket, helmet, and a single oar, and then tells us the basics. We sit on the sides of the raft, rather than in the middle. Half of us are rowing to the right, the other half row to the left. When we are in the calm water, he gives us some more training so we know when to row. It is important to pay attention to this instruction so we know how to respond when the river is not calm. When we hit the rapids, sitting in the middle of the raft, expertly commanding the oars, he directs the boat and shouts instructions for us to follow. Each side rows only when he tells us to. We paddle either forward or backward, depending on his instructions, which are based on his deep knowledge of the river.

In the thirty years I have been rafting, I have never had a guide tell us to do the wrong thing. Also unheard of is a rafter choosing to argue with the guide, or do the opposite of what he says. Given the dangerous nature of what we are doing, the novice abilities of the majority of participating rafters, and the fact that the first thing you do when you show up is sign a "hold harmless" release, people just seem to "get it."

In the river of life, however, we sometimes miss the opportunity to do the right things and make the choices that would ultimately keep us safe. Instead of paying attention to the guide (God) by reading the Bible and doing what it says, we try to strike out on our own. We judge the river as always safe (believing lies); our skill level as high enough (pride); or we want to sit in on the perch and direct the boat and the other rafters (pride again). Maybe we refuse the safety equipment (following His Word, the Bible) and when the rough water hits, we have nothing to hold on to, and we find ourselves in trouble. We fail to follow His advice when the waters of life are calm. Therefore, we do not know the simple, foundational behaviors that create relationship with Him that girds us with safety and comfort when we find ourselves in the rapids.

One time many years ago, a rafter fell out of the boat after we crossed a dangerous rapid. Because he wore the safety equipment, he immediately floated to the top of the water uninjured. Our guide directed our rowing, while shouting directions to the estranged rafter. We retrieved our friend easily, but not without opportunity for disaster. Had he chosen to not listen to the guide, he might have drowned. The guide shouted at him to stop swimming against the current toward shore. He then told him to turn around and let the current carry him, and start stroking toward the middle of the river, where we would be soon. In the boat, we could easily see this was the best course of action. The plan was obvious to us: we would paddle toward him and pick him up.

Our friend, however, hesitated a moment before complying. He told us later that he wanted to fight the current and swim toward shore instead of head out toward the middle of the calmer, but still rushing, river past the rapids. He said the river scared him when he found himself in the middle of it, and he wanted nothing more to do with it. Contrary to his natural desire, however, he chose to do what the guide said (submit), and we easily got close enough to him to grab him. During all of this, I glanced at the guide, and noticed he was watching the river and our friend, while rowing the boat with all his strength. Confident in his experience and knowledge, he did not seem concerned in the least.

Like the child who falls and briefly glances at Mom to check her level of concern before reacting, I checked the guide's face to see how concerned I should be about our water-bobbing friend. The guide's calm demeanor gave me courage.

When my children were little and afraid or uncertain about something, I told them, "I know you can do this—take my courage," and they would run off and do the thing they were previously afraid of doing. When my children dealt with block towers that fell, spilled milk, mocking kids, dying pets, or friends who behaved badly, I responded with empathy and then said, "I knew that was possible. I'm not surprised. What did you learn?" and they found courage again when they did not have their own.

We need to remember that our God is omniscient, never surprised and always understanding. He is empathetic, but unflappable. We can take courage in whatever circumstances we encounter because of this aspect of His character.

"May the God of hope fill you with all joy and peace as you trust in Him, so that you may overflow with hope by the power of the Holy Spirit." (Romans 15:13 NIV)

The key part of the above verse is "as you trust in Him," because *it is to the level we trust in God that we will submit to (obey) His Word*. To the level that we trust, we will have that amount of hope. To the level of hope we then have, we will receive that amount of joy and peace through the Holy Spirit.

Do I trust God even though modern Bible scholars debate the specifics of women's roles? Yes. Can I submit to God's authority and even my husband's in the rare circumstances where we cannot meet in agreement on a decision? Yes. God is omniscient, which means that He knew ahead of time that our culture would have these understandings of the texts and be disagreeing about them. He has placed me in this day and age for a reason, and while people continue the discussion, I can move forward in the discovery of my own relationship with Him, trusting that He has it all covered, even if I do not understand it all yet.

An underlying theme in many of Max Lucado's books is that we will not understand the good that God has designed in this life (which would include marriage) until we understand who we are in Christ and gain our identity from Him. When we come to believe God's thoughts of us, it helps us interact with our husbands (and others) in a healthy way, regardless of the way they are acting.

And regardless of any man-made labels we put on our marriages, until our husbands gain some or all of their identity from Christ, no amount of love, respect, or submission from us will affect them the way only God can. Most men will positively respond to a wife's submission and respect by loving her more gently and deeply. Some, however, do not. This is not ours to change—God has a plan He is executing with our husbands and the timing is His. God does not waste anything either. He will use the time it takes to teach our husbands as an opportunity to teach us more, as well. We need to stop thinking there is an arrival point of "bliss" for us in marriage and recognize that it is all about the actual journey – not the destination. We will be growing our entire time on earth in learning to love others and love God well.

The more I have studied the topic of submission the more interesting I find it. And I confess, when I first heard about the topic, it made me angry. It made me doubt God. It made me angry at Him and at the leader of the class who taught me about what the Bible said. I thought I was giving something up. But if we study creation, we learn something: God wired men differently than He wired women.

The average man's brain is wired to be on the lookout for perceived threats more than the average woman's brain is.

I am raising two boys and I have seen this play out in ways that neither my daughter nor I ever would have considered. My young men tell me that when they enter a building, they are concerned with where the attack might come from, how they would protect those with them, and how they could get us all out. These are things the average girl doesn't process similarly. Girls will get concerned about their own safety in a dark parking lot on the way to their car, but men think about possible threats in most circumstances they are in.

And when we treat men with RESPECT that helps communicate that we are not attacking them at the moment. However, it still feels pretty similar to what he deals with all day at work, where he's wondering if someone's going to attack him, in a place where he already feels inadequate.

So yes, we need to be respectful, because the Bible tells us to do that, too. But we also must add submission to our communication repertoire because of a simple reason: To a man, "submission" is a "white flag" saying, "I'm not here to fight with you, ever. I receive you as a person, even if I might sometimes disagree with what you say." It is an attitude, a gentleness of response regardless of what he says or how he says it. It is respect on steroids.

If he's standing there, waiting for an attack, but we communicate with a white flag, he will relax. So instead of putting him on the defense, we help the two of us stay on the same team. If we are submissive first, wouldn't that then disarm our guy?

Respect is common to men, awesome, and communicates, "I'm not threatening you now." At work, there is often an assumed, "but I might be later..." lurking in the back of a man's mind. But submission? Submission communicates clearly, "There is no threat here ever."

God knows how He wired men. So He gives us great advice in how to communicate with them.

We want our marriages to reflect Christ's relationship with the church, but we need spiritually mature wives and husbands for this to take place. Maybe you have become aware of your lack of respect, friendship, submission, help, or love toward your husband. Maybe you have worked hard to change and be obedient to God. Those are good things and bring blessing to you. Know this, however: until God intervenes in your husband's life as He has in yours, and your husband responds to God the same way you have—out of repentance, love, and obedience—your marriage will not be one where the world sees Christ's loving and gentle relationship with His respectful loving church.

God will be teaching you the spiritual benefit of being long-suffering and garnering your identity from only Him in full worship with your life, while He works in your husband's heart. God also may call you to confront your husband's sin in the midst of this process.

The most important things you can do is stay focused on living life for the Audience of One and pray for yourself and your husband—not to change your husband, but rather that He will come to know the Lord on a deeper level. Most of the wives we talk to say they thought God needed to change their husbands, but it was them who also needed continued change. I have found this true for myself. *We may be committing the sin of pride by thinking we are farther along in our walk than our husbands are.*

You can, however, not only survive, but *thrive* in a marital relationship where your spouse does not "get it," or even neglects you. I realize that is a politically incorrect statement to make. I also realize how painful marriage can be. The evidence is in, however, and it states that God can more than fulfill your needs. God has chosen you and will not ever leave you. Know that if you are in a desolate marriage, God means it for good. You may have to go through some difficulties with your husband, but trust that God means it for good.

"And we know that for those who love God all things work together for good, for those who are called according to his purpose." (Romans 8:28 ESV)

"No, I will not abandon you as orphans—I will come to you." (John 14:18 NLT)

"You are my friends if you obey me. I no longer call you servants, because a master doesn't confide in his servants. Now you are my friends, since I have told you everything the Father told me. You didn't choose me, I chose you. I appointed you to go and produce fruit that will last, so that the Father will give you whatever you ask for, using my name. I command you to love each other." (John 15:14-17 NLT)

"Look at the birds of the air: they neither sow nor reap nor gather into barns, and yet your heavenly Father feeds them. Are you not of more value than they?" (Matthew 6:26 ESV)

"You are the light of the world—like a city on a mountain, glowing in the night for all to see. Don't hide your light under a basket! Instead, put it on a stand and let it shine for all. In the same way, let your good deeds shine out for all to see, so that everyone will praise your heavenly Father." (Matthew 5:14–16 NLT)

The promise in 1 Peter 3:1–2 (that our husbands who do not know Christ will come to know Him, due in part from our behavior) has come to life in many women's marriages. A friend of mine ran several studies using *The Respect Dare for Married Women,* and one of the participants shared how she was led only by the Holy Spirit regarding how to respect her husband without any assistance from another human. Many of the exercises in the book were familiar to her, even though she had never seen it before.
Her husband had been aggressive and condemning of her relationship with Christ yet she continued to turn the other cheek.[32] She walked closely with God, listening and obeying the cues of the Holy Spirit, not mentored or helped by any other materials or women in her life. Her husband ended up weeping, confessing to her that he was sorry for how he had treated her and that he was amazed at her responding in love toward him all those years. He then asked how he could become a Christian. They met with her pastor that day, and her husband began his journey of faith. They are still married, and both are growing.

Another woman wrote to me to let me know she had left her husband for a week. He had been verbally abusing her

---

[32] Luke 6:29

and her son for many years. She had "done all the things" in that she had lovingly confronted him. He became even angrier so she took him to another Christian man to confront him. This is step two in the Matthew 18 approach to conflict. The other Christian also happened to be a pastor, thus she felt she simultaneously worked through step three of Matthew 18. Her husband did not stop being aggressive to her and her children and she realized that she was dealing with a fool instead of a wise man. She did not want to leave, but sensed God directing her to. She learned through 1 Corinthians 7:10–11[33] that she should aim to not divorce (the literal meaning of "separate" in the verse in the original language) but if she did, it was to be for the purpose of restoring the marriage. God used her leaving to get her husband's attention and he was ready to work on his end of things for the first time. They also are still married and moving forward.

When I think of the video of Sarah, from Voice of the Martyrs,[34] I am humbled at the incredible strength of her relationship with Jesus. As editor of an underground Christian paper, she was captured and tortured. Her captors made her walk for hours, shackled, until her ankles bled. She was beaten in an attempt to glean the names of others who worked with her. A man put out his cigarette on her arm. She lives in China.

I stand in awe of the faith of these women who suffer verbal and physical abuse for the cause of Christ, and

---

[33] 10 To the married I give this command (not I, but the Lord): A wife must not separate from her husband. 11 But if she does, she must remain unmarried or else be reconciled to her husband. And a husband must not divor
ce his wife.
[34] http://www.youtube.com/watch?v=yDHWYK_HtRg

some suffering from the hands of the men they have married. I want to tell them to, "Get out! Save yourselves!" In doing so, I would be challenging their relationship with God because some have told me they feel led to do what they are doing. Who am I to question their relationship with God when it provides them with such incredible strength? These women have shared the stories of how they called the police, after gently asking him not to be harsh with their child, and he assaulted them both. They tell me how God encouraged them to forgive him, led some to separate, and others to return. I marvel at the depth of their reliance on our Lord, the intimacy with which he heals their wounds and encourages them to be women of strength and dignity, communicating with them about what to do next repetitively throughout the day. I feel privileged to pray for each one of them. To say that there is but one answer would fly in the face of everything I believe about God and diminish their sacrifice and faith, whether they have separated or whether they have stayed.

Understand, however, that the accepted behaviors of abuse from a man are seen if he calls you names, hits you, shakes you, pushes you, threatens you, forces you to have sex when you are sick or exhausted, blocks you from leaving a room, withholds affection or neglects you, controls how you spend money, demeans you, regards you with contempt or disgust, refuses to allow you access to people, places, or money; and many other behaviors[35]; and his behaviors are sin. If you allow this to continue in your home, you are creating a lasting imprint for your children about what unhealthy relationships look like. If

---

[35] Please get help if you are dealing with these situations. http://www.cdh.org/medical-services/services-A-Z/emergency/domestic-abuse/abusive-behavior-checklist.aspx

you allow him to treat your children abusively, you are a party to the abuse. You have an obligation to God and your children and must protect them because they cannot protect themselves.[36] Continuing to do nothing does not bring your husband good, but rather encourages him to continue in his sin.

I also know women who have followed Matthew 18[37] and confronted their husband's sin and been met with difficulty each step of the way. Through persevering, however, most of them have seen their marriages taken to new heights of tenderness, intimacy, and glory for God. One woman's husband turned away from pornography and became a follower of Christ as a result of her gentle confrontation through all the steps outlined in Matthew 18. He wrote to me and I featured him on my blog – search up "pornography" and you'll come across his story. I still tear up thinking about what God did in their marriage. Sometimes He says to confront. Sometimes He says to ignore an insult or turn the other cheek. This is a sacred path, a journey paved with tears – and one we cannot possibly prescribe specifically for others.

---

[36] Leslie Varnick's book, "*The Emotionally Destructive Relationship,*" is extremely helpful in helping you think correctly about your relationship. Leslie Barner's book, "*A Way of Hope,*" gives you the steps to move forward.

[37] Matthew 18:15-20 (NLT) If another believer sins against you, go privately and point out the fault. If the other person listens and confesses it, you have won that person back. But if you are unsuccessful, take one or two others with you and go back again, so that everything you say may be confirmed by two or three witnesses. If that person still refuses to listen, take your case to the church. If the church decides you are right, but the other person won't accept it, treat that person as a pagan or a corrupt tax collector.

Perhaps one can best think about submission by first understanding what it is not. Based on Biblical truth, here is a list of myths we have put together:

- *Submissive wives are stupid, irresponsible, weak, and passive women who need to be taken care of by men.* Many women who are submissive wives have the ability to multitask, connect deeply with others, and handle both analytical and nonlinear processes simultaneously.

- *Submissive wives are invisible in their homes or elsewhere.* Someone once asked me about the lifestyle I had chosen, wondering how I dealt with "not having a voice." I had no idea what he was talking about because my voice is always taken into account.

- *Submissive wives are women who spend all their time waiting on their husbands to tell them what to do.* We were competent when we married, why would we cease handling responsibility?

- *Submissive wives always protect their husbands so they do not have to deal with problems.* Marital Math is 1 + 1 = 1 (remember "one flesh" from Genesis). Let your husband be responsible for his decisions. For example, allow him to interact with his children, even when they are behaving badly. Sometimes you may take care of the issues yourself so he can rest, particularly if he has had a bad day.

- *Submissive wives always allow others to fail.* We are supposed to help our husbands. It is wise to have the discernment to know when to offer up a, "I don't know if this will help you, but when I ran carpool for soccer, the route I took was . . . to save time." Having said that, sometimes our husband will disagree or not be mature enough to accept help, so know it is okay to allow him to learn by experiencing the consequences of a decision. It also is possible you don't know everything and his solution addresses the problem more adequately. Be mature enough to be okay with that. If you can, you often will find the two of you work out "God's best" as a combination of both of your ideas.

- *Submissive wives ask their husbands for decisions on literally everything.* Sorry, no. I can think of few ways to quickly drive a husband crazy than suddenly becoming incompetent.

- *Submissive wives think the "helper" role means knowing how to solve his problems and then manipulating him toward specific action.* If your husband asks for your advice, let him know what you think, especially if it is in an area of your expertise. If it is not, encourage him to seek out the advice of another man with more experience. Know that the more you encourage him to connect with other men, the more he will value your opinion.

- *Submissive wives constantly give their husbands advice when not asked for it, in an effort to "help" him.* If you have something really important that he needs to know, tell him, "I'm not sure this would be of any benefit to you, and I'm not even sure it would work, but one thing I've noticed when dealing with... is..." That is a basic "cushioning" of instructional or potentially disagreeable communication—it's a method used in business all the time and is considered respectful.

- *Submissive wives do not give input, even when asked, applying the "quiet and gentle spirit" admonishment to extremes.* Our husbands need us to be their friends. That means having discernment and not withholding information.

• • •

- *Submissive wives have to do whatever their husbands say, even if it is sinful, because they are under their husband's authority.* No. We serve God first. We have the freedom to refuse if our husband and God are in conflict with something. Be assured that our God loves us and protects us, just as He did Sarah, who was taken from Abraham, her husband, and given over to the harem of the king not once, but twice![38] Are we that close to the Father to know what He wants us to do, and then do it, no matter how crazy or dangerous it might sound?

- *Submissive wives know our role is only that of "maid" or "slave" to the whims of the family members.* Submissive wives are women of strength and dignity, with interests of their own, activities they enjoy, and friends they want to spend time with. They encourage their families to understand "the preciousness of others," regardless of their gender, including themselves. They train their children to have life skills. This means children need chores to do at home, which then means the wives are not doing every bit of

---

[38] Genesis 12:10-20 and Genesis 20:1-18   Scholars differ on what actually happened to Sarah. In the first account, Pharoah is punished with diseases on him and his household, and chastises Abraham. He pays Abraham, as well. Some scholars believe that Sarah would have been taken regardless of whether or not Abraham had called her his sister instead of his wife. Times as they were, the prevailing question was not whether or not she would be taken, but rather instead, would Abraham be killed? As her brother the odds were less likely that he would die. The second time she was taken, God protected Abimelech (and Sarah) by sending him a dream in which he revealed Sarah was Abraham's wife. The second time it is clear that the king did not have sexual relations with her. In the first, it is not known. The events take place twenty-five years apart, according to some scholars.

manual labor. They sometimes work alongside their children, and other times, children complete the tasks on their own. Submissive wives remember they are equal heirs to the throne and made in God's own image!

- *Submissive wives rely on their husband's relationship with God instead of developing their own.* Wives need their own relationships with God.

Someone asked on my blog if "submissive wives ever miss their freedom" and if they "have any rights or privileges or just do as the husband commands?" Honestly, the questions made me sad because of the depth of the misunderstanding. God never treated Eve as the property of Adam. Granted, in ancient times, women were considered property in some cultures by men. When Jesus Christ arrived, he turned the world upside down by not only teaching women, but also by engaging in dialogue with them, going out of His way to meet with them (the woman at the well in Samaria), and even declared His deity to a woman first.

We spend way too much time fussing about this topic, in my opinion. "Submission" is merely an active choice to view our husbands as the CEO's of our families. Wives are the "Presidents." If we still disagree about an issue after we have discussed it (even more than once, as long as we're not disrespectful or contentious), the submissive wife then defers to her husband's judgment, because at the end of the day, he's held accountable. Failing to voice an opinion can often lead to enabling unhealthy behaviors if they already exist in the marriage.

I do not agree with everything my husband says and he wants my opinion when I disagree. However, sometimes *people* (not just wives) can be just plain disagreeable, which consistently arouses resentment and causes conflict. You know the people I am talking about—maybe it is the guy in the next office cube or the woman three houses down from you—these people would argue about anything, just like your toddler (or teenager) who is trying to establish independence. At their core, they are oppositional as people – don't be one of them! You could say that the sky is blue and these folks would find some way of disagreeing with what you said.

Being argumentative is evidence of poor communication skills and disrespect – and it is the proof of foolishness. Being defensive is a reflection of a lack of maturity – and again is the proof of foolishness. Mature wise women are not threatened by the opinions of others. Being submissive has everything to do with a simple understanding of who is held responsible and nothing to do with being considered "less" than someone else. People who argue over everything and respond defensively are difficult to get along with, regardless of what gender they are. This is also called being "contentious" in the Bible.

"If anyone is inclined to be contentious, we have no such practice, nor do the churches of God." (1 Corinthians 11:16 ESV)

"It is better to dwell in a desert land, than with a contentious and fretful woman." (Proverbs 21:19 ASV)

Choosing to be submissive as a wife is essentially exactly that—a choice. You can choose willingly to place yourself under your husband's leadership, regardless of how good he is at it, or you can choose not to. The selection you make depends entirely on the level in which you trust God.

If you trust Him a lot, choosing the vice-president's spot instead of president should be a relatively easy concept. If you trust Him little, obviously you will struggle with this more.

Regardless, submission is a choice a wife makes willingly, and it does not conflict with what the Bible says. I read online recently a pastor's blog who literally said that "wives are to submit to their husbands in the Lord in everything literally means 'in everything' even pornography, wife-swapping, cheating on your taxes."

If you think submission makes you a doormat and that you have nothing to contribute to your marriage that is a choice you can make. I don't believe that is what God's Word teaches, but there are plenty of people out there that want you to believe that it does. And I understand – sometimes it is just easier to just let someone else be in charge of everything and just go along with it. In the short term, it really can be easier, but in the long, it often does not yield fruit and can cause all sorts of other problems.

Obviously, Sapphira (from the book of Acts, chapter 5, in the Bible) wasn't off the hook for doing what was right, even if her husband told her to do it, and neither are we. Unfortunately, I didn't realize that God's Word doesn't teach blind obedience for wives, but submission – it's different.

And I am hoping I realized this soon enough. When your kids are little, it doesn't seem to matter as much, but when they are older, you wonder if there's been enough proper modeling going on. Do I want my sons thinking a certain way about women? Or behaving certain ways towards them? Or seeing Sapphira behavior? It appears

Acts 5 tells a different story from the model of "submission=obedience" that so many people would like to subscribe to. Sapphira obeyed her husband. She, like him, lied about how much money they received for selling some land.

It's not by coincidence that it is Peter she lied to – and Peter who later tells wives to submit. I often wonder what might have happened if she instead had said to her husband, "Baby, I know you mean well, but we can't sin against God – we can't lie. I know you are a man of integrity, and I know how tempting this is, but let's just tell the truth here." But we wouldn't have her example to learn from if she'd done the right thing, now would we?

Don't misconstrue 1 Peter 3:6 into an absolute – it says, literally, "just as Sarah obeyed Abraham, calling him lord, and you have become her children if you do what is right without being frightened by any fear." We often miss the connection to Hebrews 11:11, where Sarah's faith is praised, "And by faith even Sarah, who was past childbearing age, was enabled to bear children because she considered him faithful who had made the promise."

To fail to acknowledge her relationship with God is to choose blind obedience to man (contrary to Acts 5:29, and all the examples of others who knew God and disobeyed their authorities – Joseph and Potiphar's wife, Esther, Abigail, just to name a few, all of which are examples to us). And let us not forget that Sarah actually suggested something her husband disagreed with, and when he struggled with it before God, the Lord told Abraham to listen to his wife and do what she said (Genesis 21:8-14).

For those using Peter's suggestion as a command, we need to remember that he also was the one that the Lord used to chastise Sapphira. And God killed her, just like He did her husband for sinning against God.

So contrary to some beliefs, "obey" is not a commanded thing for wives in the Bible. Submission, which is willing, IS commanded for those whose husbands are in alignment with God's will.

One night when my college-age son and husband were discussing something and it got out of hand, I did what I sensed God wanted me to do. I stepped in and gently said, "Hey guys? Look. I know you both love and respect each other, but that's not showing up right now. You both need to take things up a notch in how you're speaking to each other. You're both better than this. Why don't you take a break for a few minutes, maybe pray about it, and then come back when you both can be calmer and just work through the issue instead of attacking each other?"

And they both agreed. My son went downstairs, and my husband stayed put.

I sat down next to him, put my hand on his shoulder and said, "Baby, this is the same advice you gave me a while back. You were so incredibly right then – and now I don't want to see you caught in this negative spin. You're a good dad. I know you want what's best for him, and he's making mistakes, but it's going to be okay. Don't own it. He's a good kid. And before he was here, there was just you and I – and it will be just you and I again. We're going to get through this." He said, "You are right. I'm letting it get to me. Thanks."

I love moments like that because it is in the middle of them that I feel most like a mom, most like a wife, most like a woman using my gifting to help two of the men I love most on the planet. Some would call what I did unsubmissive.

We call it being helpful in our home.

How About You?

1. *What lies have you believed about submission as it pertains to your marriage? What is different now for you?*

2. *Is your marriage one-sided in any way? Are you living with a gentle, loving, kind-hearted man whom you respond to with contempt, disrespect, and a lack of loving submission? Have you been obeying God for many years and are still dealing with a hard-hearted man who behaves unlovingly toward you? Are things somewhere in between?*
3. *Take a few moments to pray, asking God to forgive you for your lack of obedience. Pray for your husband to grow deeper in his walk with God. Pray for your marriage to be one that represents Christ's loving, gentle leadership of a loving church.*

Chapter Dares:

Dare 1: Continue practicing silence, apologizing, and forgiving in your communication repertoire. *Encourage others with what you say to them, focusing on the positives and not the negatives. Get rid of criticism, contempt, defensiveness, and stonewalling.*

Dare 2: Continue to create opportunities to intentionally submit to your husband. *Note: If you are concerned that you may be a "doormat" or not have healthy boundaries in your marriage, please sign up for the Strength & Dignity eCourse on my blog. You'll learn to respect yourself, others, and deepen your relationship with God even more.

Dare 3: Daily choose to be interested in your husband's world, regardless of whether or not he is interested in yours. *This means the following:*

- *Become a student of the man you married, and a warrior on his behalf by asking him, "What can I pray about for you today?" This is one of the best things you can do for your relationship.*
- *Follow up at the end of the day and ask him how things went for him.*
- *Be a respectful listener when he is speaking and ask questions, encouraging him to open up about himself by*
  - *facing him*
  - *making eye contact*
  - *stopping what you are doing, if possible*
  - *not interrupting him and correcting your children if they interrupt him, then asking him to continue*
  - *nodding your head with interest*
  - *asking questions that cannot be answered with yes or no, but are open ended in nature*
  - *not offering advice unless asked, but instead empathizing with his struggles, for example: "Honey that has got to be hard for you. I'll certainly pray about that situation."*
  - *not offering an opinion on what he shares unless it is supportive or encouraging*

o *putting down your phone or looking away from the computer when he is speaking — stop multitasking*

Dare 4: Compliment his character while listening to him, *for example: "John, I love how you handled that! They certainly picked a reliable person [him] to head up that project."*

Actively choose to not get discouraged if he does not want to talk with you, displays poor listening skills, or does not want to participate. Do what you can, listen to God—His advice trumps mine always!

Remember that discouragement is steeped in lies—it's one of the calling cards of the enemy. Yes, we will discuss asking your husband for something—the second book in this series will cover that.

As you read through these dares, which pose a challenge to you? How will you meet that challenge?

What do you need God's help with? Write out your prayer requests in your journal. :

Truth #10:

The Extent to Which We Receive God's Great Love for Us Impacts How We Love & Respect Ourselves and Others

I remember when a friend's eleven-year-old son, enraged by my daughter and his sister's teasing and mocking, screamed at them, "I just want you to respect me!"

Respect is a huge issue for men. Research done by Shaunti Feldhahn in 2006 essentially shows that men frequently wonder about their abilities, and because they know this about themselves and others, they treat each other with respect. They do not challenge each other overtly. They verbally treat each other with honor. They tend not to disrespect one another.

Following is a list of what *dis*respect looks like (be sure to add the "you idiot!" tone of voice):

- Asking questions that you really don't want answered, just pointing out how stupid you think he is, like, "How could you possibly think or do XYZ . . . ?"
- Rolling your eyes with irritation or, worse, contempt
- Interrupting

- Pursing your lips and scowling as he contributes his thoughts
- Never acknowledging his ideas
- Not asking questions about what he thinks
- Starting all questions with "Why did you . . .?" because *why* is a word men use to challenge each other
- Withholding compliments instead of looking for opportunities to build him up
- Leaving him with a list of things to accomplish when you go somewhere and then criticizing him for not getting it all done
- Correcting him when he's interacting with the kids—especially if it is his first time doing something
- Disrespecting yourself, allowing the kids or him to treat you badly without saying anything about it (respect is only worth as much as it is worth to you)
- Criticizing him instead of praising him first when you have something constructive to say to him
- Expecting him to read your mind the way your sisters, girlfriends, and mother can
- Saying really helpful things like, "If you don't know, I'm not going to tell you"
- Answering for him when he's asked a question
- Mocking him
- Worse yet: mocking him in front of others
- Discounting his contribution in front of others
- Arguing with his ideas and suggestions
- Telling him how he feels or what he thinks, for example: "You think I'm . . ." or "You are angry because . . ."
- Not pursuing him. And making sure you say, "Not tonight"

The first step to respect is praying that God will change our hearts. Changing our behaviors is nice, but unless we do the hard work of becoming humble, we will not see our husbands as precious to God, as men needing respect as much as we need love. Our hearts need to be changed to avoid feeling resentful. Our failure to address our husband's sin also causes resentment. Let's ask God together to change our hearts and continue this work. Psychologists tell us that sometimes behavior comes before heart change and sometimes it's the other way around. What we think about plays a huge role in this, so I urge you to take every thought captive when thinking about your husband.

To make some behavior changes, while God is working on our hearts, however, we can start with things as simple as removing some bad communication habits. Criticism, contempt, condescension, disgust, and reflex-disagreement (when our response to anything is negative and argumentative) are all bad habits that develop over time. Respect is the opposite of these negative patterns, and both can be easily communicated verbally as well as nonverbally. It means ditching the sarcasm. It means stopping the criticism and no longer poking fun at your man, as if he were a person without feelings. *It means treating him as if he is a prized possession of God Himself, which he is, whether or not he behaves that way.*

I remind myself of these things by choosing to be respectful with all people, not just my husband, and including my children. Many conflicts with our teenagers could be avoided if we simply treated them respectfully. I try not to do things to them that I would not like done to me. I apologize when I am wrong or hurt their feelings, even inadvertently, and when I am overly demanding. As a mom and Sunday school teacher, I often called the boys in my life, "sir," even when they were young. It did not diminish my authority as their mother and primary teacher in any way. It did help me remember how much God values them.

Many times I am asked for a list of what respectful behaviors are. I have a list of 101 on my blog, but here are just a few:

1. Refrain from interrupting him in conversation. Men and women interrupt differently – women interrupt to communicate empathy, but men do it to dominate.

2. Make eye contact while listening to him.

3. Avoid rolling your eyes while speaking with him. This communicates that you think his ideas are stupid – he'll stop sharing what he thinks with you if you keep responding this way.

4. Smile pleasantly while conversing with him.

5. Respect yourself and have healthy boundaries because if you don't, your respect for him means nothing to him. The worse you allow yourself to be treated, the more sin you tolerate towards your children or yourself, the less you help him be a better man.

6. Appear approachable instead of judgmental while listening, asking questions to further your understanding, even if you think you might disagree.

7. Avoid pursing your lips and scowling while speaking to him.

8. Understand his point of view when you disagree, knowing that even though he may not be communicating emotionally, he might feel strongly about his thoughts.

9. Affirm his point of view, especially when you disagree.

10. Do something he likes to do with him.

11. Help him carve out time to spend with his friends.

12. Choose carefully whether or not the issue at hand is worthy of disagreement – the more you disagree with him, the less he values your input.

13. When a course of action is decided upon, support the decision enthusiastically instead of begrudgingly.

14. If you disagree with a position he holds, after understanding and affirming it ("If I understand you correctly, you are saying…I can see why you would say that because…") let him know you have another thought ("A concern I have about this is," or, "What I am wondering is," "What I'm struggling with is…").

15. When having difficult communication, treat him gently. Soften your disagreement with cushioning statements.

16. Don't take it personally when he commits an oversight – his mind is probably on something else and he isn't focused or forgot.

17. Say, "Thank you!" when he does something for you, regardless of what it is – wise women are appreciative of all things. Anyone can be grateful for big things, a wise woman is grateful for the small also.

18. Say, "Thank you for going to work," or "Thank you for looking for work today," if he is doing either. Wise people thank others for doing the things they do daily instead of taking them for granted.

19. When you ask for something say, "Would you please..." Wise people do not assume attitudes of entitlement, but rather understand the preciousness of others to God and treat others accordingly, instead of taking them for granted.

20. Don't argue with any act of generosity he displays, even if you think it is not necessary, or if it's for you and you don't think you need it. Accept his generosity.

21. Compliment him on acts of generosity, "You are so generous! Thank you for doing that."

22. Don't correct his efforts in diapering, feeding, or playing with the baby, unless there is a significant safety risk involved. If he wants help, he will ask you for it.

23. Have emotional control when you bring up issues.

24. Understand that talking about issues when you are upset does not yield the best result for either of you.

25. Don't get frustrated with him when he doesn't express his feelings well.

26. Accept his feelings and affirm him for sharing them, even if you don't agree with his position ("That sounds like it is a difficult thing for you...I appreciate your sharing this with me. How can I help?").

27. Don't talk about issues when he is tired, distracted, or hungry.

28. Don't assume he has a negative feeling, instead, tell him, "I'm sure you have a good reason for what you are saying, can you share with me what it is? I'm confused."

29. Don't ask questions beginning with the word, "Why?" Research done by Shaunti Feldhahn indicates this is a challenge word to most men.[39]

30. Say, "Excuse me," when you are trying to get his attention, or say his name.

31. Don't just launch into conversation, say his name and then ask if he has a few minutes to talk about something.

---

[39] The Male Factor, Shaunti Feldhahn, 2011

32. If he does not have time now, ask him if later would be better, or if he would suggest a time that works for him.

33. Introduce him to people at social gatherings, even if he's already met them, unless they are very good friends of yours whom he sees frequently. "David, I think you've met my friend, Sarah." This helps him feel more comfortable in social situations with you.

34. Apologize by saying, "I'm sorry I did XYZ. I feel terrible that I ABC and will try not to do it again."

35. Don't be disagreeable in the way you disagree. Choose carefully what you will argue about.

36. Actively agree with him frequently, saying, "You are right! That's a great insight."

37. Learn how your stuff from your childhood affects your perceptions and continue to work through those things to grow.

38. Contact him via email or text to let him know you are praying for him – check to see if he has any specific requests today.

39. Initiate intimacy.

40. Cultivate your own relationship with God.

41. Take care of yourself physically – get rest, exercise, and eat right.

42. Find out what "domestic support" looks like to him and do the stuff that matters to him.

43. Smile and greet him when you first see him and when he comes home from work (or you do).

44. Let him finish his sentences without interrupting and without finishing them for him.

45. Ask him what he thinks about stuff that's important to you or the kids.

46. Stop what you are doing when he is talking and make eye contact with him, being a good listener by being interested in what he is saying.

47. Give him at least one compliment a day that builds him up – point out a character strength and say why it matters.

48. Be enthusiastic about intimacy, pursuing him.

49. Encourage him to spend time with his friends, and make it easy for him to do so.

50. Touch him when you are speaking to him. There is a ton of power in a person's touch. Research shows it improves brain function, releases feel-good hormones, and can help you and others feel more connected.

While we are talking about how valuable respect is to men, we need to remember to treat our girlfriends and ourselves with respect and love.

I also call women "gorgeous" or "beautiful" for the same reasons. I apologize if that offends you, but I believe all women are beautiful to God, and they are to me, too, regardless of how they look. When I see wrinkles and dark circles around a woman's eyes, instead of fatigue, I see a life of service and smiling. It's lovely to me. Frankly, I don't think we get told that we are beautiful enough. I started doing this after my firstborn son's pediatrician greeted me with a "Hey gorgeous!" at our first well-baby visit.

I was a mess. Spit-up stains on my shoulder, hair barely done, no makeup, and this doctor woman called me "gorgeous." I said, "Why on earth would you say that?" She said, "Every mother is beautiful." I thought long and hard about that. The extra pounds, the sagging skin, the haggard look, and I was beautiful. And I believed it. In that moment, I knew God smiled down on my tired, lumpy body, leaking breasts, dark-circled eyes, and He was pleased. What woman do you know needs to be reminded that she's beautiful? I think we all do.

Believing that the Creator of the Universe values me deeply helps me serve Him as King, even when I do not fully understand the lesson at hand. The contexts of marriage and mothering obviously provide numerous opportunities to further explore our identity in Him. My favorite testimonies include a wife coming closer to finding her full identity in Christ, taking a step along the journey of desiring only Him, which always results in a deeper trust of our Lord and a higher ability to love others well.

We all have to come to terms with our level or lack of trust in God. No matter how long we live on this earth, we will struggle with obeying and believing Him 100 percent of the time. The voice of the world is loud, as are the voices of our own desires, and either easily distract us. Because our interactions are with other fallible humans, we forget to trust His great love for us. We expect Christians to behave perfectly. We put unrealistic expectations upon them. We judge God by the behavior of other humans. That negatively impacts our trust in Him, though it should not. We do not completely believe He is for us, and, as a result, struggle with submitting to Him.

"No, in all these things we are more than conquerors through him who loved us. For I am sure that neither death nor life, nor angels nor rulers, nor things present nor things to come, nor powers, nor height nor depth, nor anything else in all creation, will be able to separate us from the love of God in Christ Jesus our Lord." (Romans 8:37–39 ESV)

Recently, a dear friend of mine, who has a vast knowledge of the Bible and has been in ministry longer than I have been alive, was lamenting to me about her inability to love others well. I reminded her of how well she knows the Bible. In a moment of frustration, she remarked about how "young I was to 'get it.'"

I asked her, "Do you know every word, in order, of the whole Bible?"

She said, "Of course not!"

I said, "But you do know more than most, right? You are always the person I call when I can't remember where to find a verse. You have most of them tucked away. I would love to have that resource in my own head! We like to compare ourselves to others, but the reality is that this side of heaven is all about learning. Learning to think like

Christ and act like Jesus, learning to love others well is like starting in Genesis, and then memorizing every word of the Bible, in order. You are born, and it is 'Ready, set, go! See how far you can get before you die.' We will never 'get there.' And no matter how far we do get, comparing ourselves to other people is pointless because they have infinity staring them in the face as well. Learning to love is just like that. We never fully get it this side of heaven— we just have to keep moving forward."

We have to learn to use the opportunities we are given. They are all about learning to let Christ's love and compassion flow out of us to the world.

How about you?

1. *Go back through the bullet-point list of disrespectful behaviors at the beginning of the chapter, marking those that are a challenge for you. If you are feeling really brave, ask either your husband or oldest child (depending on age – tween and up is best) to let you know which of those are present in your repertoire. What behaviors do you need to work on?*

2. *How about the list for respectful behaviors? Were there any that you do well? How respectful of a person are you in general?*

3. *How respectful are you of people other than your husband? Do you treat children with respect? Do you treat acquaintances or coworkers better than your family? What is God revealing to you?*

4. How is our identity in Christ related to respecting our husbands and the other people in our lives?

Chapter Dares:

Dare 1: Make a list of all the strengths and talents God has given you. *Thank Him for these things. Ask Him to show you how to develop them further, for His glory. If you struggle with feelings of self-worth, ask God to reveal to you the lies you believe about yourself and help you to see His truth of who He made you to be. Look up Jeremiah 29:11 and write it on a card. Tape the card to your mirror or put it in your Bible, along with the list of strengths, and ask God to help you be the person He created you to be every day.*

Dare 2: Review the following scriptures daily for at least a week, preferably 21 days, highlighting those that speak to you personally:

My Identity in Jesus Christ

I am God's child. *"Yet to all who received him, to those who believed in his name, he gave the right to become children of God."* (John 1:12)

I am Jesus Christ's friend. *"I no longer call you servants, because a servant does not know his master's business. Instead, I have called you friends, for everything that I learned from my Father I have made known to you."* (John 15:15)

I am one with God. *"But he who unites himself with the Lord is one with him in spirit."* (1 Corinthians 6:17)

I am worth a great price and have been purchased with God's own Son. *"Do you not know that your body is a temple of the Holy Spirit, who is in you, whom you have received from God? You are not your own; you were bought at a price. Therefore honor God with your body."* (1 Corinthians 6:19–20)

I am pursued, sought after, precious, honored, loved, wooed, and worthy of nations by the Lover of my soul, the One who knows me, who created me, the One who formed me. *"But now, this is what the LORD says—he who created you, Jacob, he who formed you, Israel: 'Do not fear, for I have redeemed you; I have summoned you by name; you are mine . . . Since you are precious and honored in my sight, and because I love you, I will give people in exchange for you, nations in exchange for your life.'"* (Isaiah 43:1, 4 NIV)

I am a member of Jesus' body, the Church. *"Now you are the body of Christ, and each one of you is a part of it."* (1 Corinthians 12:27)

I have been specially chosen by God, adopted into His family, redeemed, and forgiven. *"Praise be to the God and Father of our Lord Jesus Christ, who has blessed us in the heavenly realms with every spiritual blessing in Christ. For he chose us in him before the creation of the world to be holy and blameless in his sight. In love he predestined us to be adopted as his sons through Jesus Christ, in accordance with his pleasure and will to the praise of his glorious grace, which he has freely given us in the One he loves. In him we have redemption through his blood, the forgiveness of sins, in accordance with the riches of God's grace that he lavished on us with all wisdom and understanding."* (Ephesians 1:3–8)

* * *

God wants to talk to me any time I want to talk to Him, and I can approach Him with confidence because of Jesus. *"Therefore, since we have a great high priest who has gone through the heavens, Jesus the Son of God, let us hold firmly to the faith we profess. For we do not have a high priest who is unable to sympathize with our weaknesses, but we have one who has been tempted in every way, just as we are yet was without sin. Let us then approach the throne of grace with confidence, so that we may receive mercy and find grace to help us in our time of need."* (Hebrews 4:14–16)

No one can judge or condemn me. *"Therefore, there is now no condemnation for those who are in Christ Jesus."* (Romans 8:1)

God has a plan for good things for me, regardless of what I am going through right now. *"And we know that in all things God works for the good of those who love him, who have been called according to his purpose."* (Romans 8:28)

God has a plan for me, listens to me, and allows me to find Him when I look for Him. *"For I know the plans I have for you,"* declares the Lord, *"plans to prosper you and not to harm you, plans to give you hope and a future. Then you will call on me and come and pray to me, and I will listen to you. You will seek me and find me when you seek me with all your heart."* (Jeremiah 29:11–13)

God started a good work in me and He will finish it. *"Being confident of this, that he who began a good work in you will carry it on to completion until the day of Christ Jesus."* (Philippians 1:6)

I have a citizenship in heaven. *"But our citizenship is in heaven. And we eagerly await a Saviour from there, the Lord Jesus Christ."* (Philippians 3:20)

My fear and lack of self-discipline are not from God. *"For God did not give us a spirit of timidity, but a spirit of power, of love and of self-discipline."* (2 Timothy 1:7)

Through Jesus, my work will have a lasting effect. *"You did not choose me, but I chose you and appointed you to go and bear fruit, fruit that will last. Then the Father will give you whatever you ask in my name."* (John 15:16)

I am the temple of the Holy Spirit. *"Don't you know that you yourselves are God's temple and that God's Spirit lives in you?"* (1 Corinthians 3:16)

I am made new and am a reconciler and ambassador for God and His people. *"Therefore, if anyone is in Christ, he is a new creation; the old has gone, the new has come! All this is from God, who reconciled us to himself through Christ and gave us the ministry of reconciliation: that God was reconciling the world to himself in Christ, not counting men's sins against them. And he has committed to us the message of reconciliation. We are therefore Christ's ambassadors, as though God were making his appeal through us. We implore you on Christ's behalf: Be reconciled to God. God made him who had no sin to be sin for us, so that in him we might become the righteousness of God."* (2 Corinthians 5:17–21)
"Therefore, if anyone is in Christ, he is a new creation; the old has gone, the new has come!" (2 Corinthians 5:17)

I am made in God's own image, and a joint heir with Christ. *"So God created mankind in his own image, in the* *image of God he created them; male and female he created them."* (Genesis 1:27)

"Because you are sons, God sent the Spirit of his Son into our hearts, the Spirit who calls out, 'Abba,' So you are no longer a slave, but a son; and since you are a son, God has made you also an heir." (Galatians 4:6–7)

"Now if we are children, then we are heirs-heirs of God and co-heirs with Christ, if indeed we share in his sufferings in order that we may also share in his glory." (Romans 8:17)

I am a saint. *"Paul, an apostle of Christ Jesus by the will of God, to the saints in Ephesus, the faithful in Christ Jesus."* (Ephesians 1:1)

"To the church of God in Corinth, to those sanctified in Christ Jesus and called to be holy, together with all those everywhere who call on the name of our Lord Jesus Christ their Lord and ours." (1 Corinthians 1:2)

I am righteous and holy. *"And to put on the new self, created to be like God in true righteousness and holiness."* (Ephesians 4:24)

I am the devil's enemy. *"Be self-controlled and alert. Your enemy the devil prowls around like a roaring lion looking for someone to devour."* (1 Peter 5:8)

Truth #11:

Wise Women Practice the Discipline of Silence – And When They Speak, it Matters!

December is a difficult month for many busy women, with the added activities of the Christmas holiday. I remember one particularly stressful Christmas Day when our daughter was three months old and her brothers were ages three and five. That evening, I found myself crawling around on the hardwood floor in our family room, cleaning up pieces of wrapping paper and packaging materials. The room looked like a tornado had hit it. Exhausted from a month of planning, preparation, and too much activity, I felt a hot lump grow in my throat. I looked at my husband reading the paper in the rocking chair. My eyes began to fill with tears. My nose began to run. Hearing my sniffing, he bent his paper over to look at me. "You okay?" he asked. At that moment, all I knew was fury. I don't think I've ever been so angry at another person in my life. I desperately needed help, but mistakenly didn't think I should have to ask for it. I couldn't speak.

After a moment, I muttered the lie, "I'm fine" and kept cleaning up. When I finished, I went upstairs and shared my rage with God. I did not know what to do. I did not know what to say to my husband. I had been studying submission and respect, and some of the teaching left me feeling utterly helpless. According to what I was reading, I was responsible for everything in the home and needed to provide my husband with a haven from his work. I should have his slippers by his chair, his newspaper ready daily, and a hot meal on the table when he came in. I was to orchestrate family life around his return, his desires, and his activities. The children were to be well-behaved accoutrements to the production.

I put tons of energy into creating the perfect environment in our home in an attempt to please God and be a stellar wife. The problem was the baby and I were passing thrush[40] back and forth, the kindergartener also had been sick and cranky, and the three-year-old had taken mess making to a new level. I also had post-partum depression. Jim had been traveling out of state quite a bit for work and we had no family in the area. I felt alone, exhausted, and devastated.

If I simply had asked Jim to help me straighten up or given him specific requests, he would have been more than willing to pitch in. But I did not ask because I thought I would be a bad wife if I did. My pride and my circumstances were at odds. I did expect him, however, to "just know" what he should do, like a girlfriend or sister would. What I didn't realize at the time was how he perceived things. Many men don't offer to help because they believe that would be communicating they don't think you can handle something. Jim thought he was letting me know he thought I could handle things—by not

---

[40] Thrush is an infection common to breastfeeding when baby or mom receives antibiotic treatment and an overgrowth of yeast occurs. It is extremely painful for both mom and baby and makes breastfeeding extremely difficult.

offering to help. Naïve in my experience, I spent the holidays furious and in silence. I hardly said a word to anyone. He asked me at one point why I wasn't talking to him and I responded, "I have nothing good to say, so I'm not saying anything."

A week of silently wrestling with God over the submission topic, Bible reading, prayer, and avoiding conflict with my husband found us at an odd place on New Year's Eve. I bravely "broke the rules" and asked Jim to help me get ready for a birthday party for one of our boys. He gladly helped and we had fun together.

Having spent the week in silence while being bombarded with the frequent temptation to lash out verbally, I came to the conclusion that I just did not understand anything about being a Christian or a good wife. I realized that, in spite of all the Bible time, I lacked the skills and the right mind-set. I begged God to help me. I had never felt like such a failure at life before. I thought, *if everything I've studied, read, and applied in the last ten years still leaves me here, I don't know what else to do.* I gave up trying to fix my marriage myself and tearfully handed it over to God.

Many of the dare-takers who write to me share something they have in common with my experience. We all have come to a place of finally submitting to God. We start living our lives for the Audience of One by beginning *with the practice of purposeful silence.*

We create noise in our lives not just through the television, the radio, or streaming music or podcasts through our computers, but also through the newspaper, books we choose to read, friends we surround ourselves with, stores where we choose to shop, checkout line magazine covers we pay attention to, and the plethora of busyness we pursue, running from one activity to the next either for our kids or ourselves. If we do not actively choose to create extended periods of time for silence, we grow deaf to the voice of our Creator.

His voice is still and small.

At some point in our walk with Him, He will stop responding to our requests for "billboards," and instead challenge us to become better listeners. For me, that Christmas week spent with barely a word to others changed my life forever. I not only heard my own black heart, but I heard God through the pages of His Word.

I had been spending daily time in His Word, but that week, I was not just spending time with Him for the purpose of learning, but also for listening.

We spend too much of our time with God rattling off requests, instead of remembering we are in the presence of the King and should be awaiting orders. As you read through today's dares, you will notice a beginning for developing our practice of purposeful silence.

We also asked you to catch your own tongue and practice adding silence to your communication behaviors for a very specific, marriage enhancing reason. Current research proves that men typically speak as many words in general as women do; however, most of a man's communication occurs at work because he feels it is purposeful.[41] Most men tend to talk less at home, where most women want

---

[41] http://www.washingtonpost.com/wp-dyn/content/article/2007/07/13/AR2007071301815.html

communication, because they are focused on relationships.

We asked you to add silence to your repertoire of communication skills because it will allow you to recognize four things:

1. Your husband may be tuning you out because of the plethora of communication if you have a habit of speaking too much.
2. If we speak respectfully, more complimentarily, and less frequently, our husbands are more likely to pay attention to what we have to say.
3. Silence gives us the space we need to formulate a respectful response when our husband says something that hurts our feelings.
4. When we speak less, we can hear God more. He always knows what we should do in any given moment. Being silent allows Him space to work in us, and in our husbands.

Hopefully you haven't filled the silence with activity on your phone. Our culture is quickly becoming one where dialogue occurs in between texts and social media posts. This doesn't help us be mindful, nor does it help us bond and connect with others, including God. Another positive impact of silence is the restraint of interruption. Most people consider it rude to interrupt another person when he or she speaking. Men view this as disrespectful, which it is. Women often interrupt to show concern.[42] We can avoid being misunderstood and be perceived as less disrespectful by not interrupting.

42

http://www.lingutronic.de/Studium/Anglistik/Gender%20Language/Gender%20Language.pdf page 9

Some of us also need to realize that we offer up advice too often and are not good listeners. We should offer advice only if asked. We have found that when we add silence to our communication skills, we become aware of some of our own thoughts. Many of these thoughts should never become spoken; they are unnecessary, often judgmental, in bad timing, and could be harmful. We can and should be more purposeful in what we do talk about and we can hear God's voice better if we will choose to actively pursue silence in our lives daily. What is really neat is creating an environment in which our husbands ask for and want our opinions and advice. This will not occur if we are a constant dripping of non-stop noise.

One of Satan's lies about wives who work at respecting their husbands has become popular and even has factions of Christianity hurling insults, calling us archaic and damaging. If you want to see how they think in greater detail, check the reviews on Amazon for *The Respect Dare for Married Women* and read the 1's and 2's. Dripping with venom, it's clear they hate the message of unconditional respect within marriage.

The lie: if you respect and submit to your husband, you have no voice in your home. You are silent. You are a doormat.

Like many of the enemy's tactics, there's a shred of truth. We are told to submit to our husbands "in everything" (Ephesians 5:22–24). This verse frequently gets twisted to mean that the wife cannot do anything without her husband's permission and is to be a robotic servant for his every whim. In assaulting the truth of this scripture, however, we lose a number of things, one of which is the discipline of silence. The practice of this discipline is a tenet of mature faith. Many proverbs speak to this:

"When words are many, sin is not absent, but he who holds his tongue is wise." (Proverbs 10:19 NIV).

"A man who lacks judgment derides his neighbor, but a man of understanding holds his tongue." (Proverbs 11:12 NIV)

"A fool shows his annoyance at once, but a prudent man overlooks an insult." (Proverbs 12:16 NIV)

"He who guards his lips guards his life, but he who speaks rashly will come to ruin." (Proverbs 13:3 NIV)

"Even a fool is thought wise if he keeps silent, and discerning if he holds his tongue." (Proverbs 17:28 NIV)

"A fool finds no pleasure in understanding, but delights in airing his own opinions." (Proverbs 18:2 NIV)

"A fool's mouth is his undoing, and his lips a snare to his soul." (Proverbs 18:6 NIV)

I could keep going, but I won't. Suffice it to say, God feels strongly about self-control when it comes to our mouths!

However, we have to see the Truth in the discipline of silence without turning it into something it is not. God is a relational Being. If I'm talking all the time, I'm not listening. So, it would stand to reason, that I should be silent with Him in order to listen to Him. My husband, as research shows is the case with the majority of men, is primarily systematic and productive rather than relational with his communication. Therefore, if I talk just to converse too often, he is apt to be unable to sort out what matters from the plethora of information. So I practice silence with him too. And for the record, I'm not saying he isn't relational. He's just not my girlfriend with whom I can go off on twenty-seven tangents before making a point.

Something we also will see in the practice of silence is the communication we have with ourselves.

"As a man thinketh, so then is he." (Proverbs 23:7 NIV)

My husband asked if I knew how to sew a button on a jacket of his. For those of you who don't sew, there's a knot you use so that it's not difficult to button. What I heard, in the silence of my head was, "Oh . . . no . . . I can't do that for him. I used up all my fine motor ability this weekend when I sewed the pocket back on our son's ski jacket . . . my hands still hurt from that—" and I responded, "I can't do that for you," and disappointment seeped into my heart. Granted, I was coming off a rather emotionally hard day, and, on top of that, my hands were still really sore. "I can ask a friend to take care of it," I said. "No, I can do it myself," he replied. "But you know how to make that knot, right?"

What I heard instead of his simple question was my own sense of inadequacy that sometimes comes along with my disabled hands. A connective tissue disorder resulting in severe early onset osteoarthritis sometimes incapacitates me. It is unpredictable, and no one knows when I am able to do things, when I'm able to do limited things, or when I'm able to barely function from the pain.

• • •

In this discussion with my husband, in my own head I heard *failure, unworthy,* and other things. And then I heard another lie: *He knows about my hands yet he wants me to do one of the most painful things, grasping a needle.* And then I heard my heart start issuing judgment his direction.

And I felt unloved.

But here's the kicker. When we talked about it later, he told me he really did just want my help. If I knew how to do it, I could tell him how to make the knot. He knew I couldn't do it and he wasn't asking me to actually use the needle.

I added all the other junk to the conversation in the middle of the silence. I had forgotten one very true tenet about men: *Most men usually say exactly what they mean. No more and no less.*

I hadn't taken him at his word.

And that, in and of itself, is disrespectful, because it doesn't give the benefit of the doubt. It is not loving behavior either.

And giving voice to that conniving, scheming enemy (or our own unhealthy feelings rooted in his lies) only creates more distance in our relationships.

So yes, practice the discipline of silence to improve your ability to hear God and communicate better with your husband (and others). Practice it with yourself, choosing carefully what words you will speak to yourself. This is respecting and loving yourself as the temple of the Holy Spirit.

Words can bring death or abundant life to all your relationships, including the one you have with yourself.

Consider for a moment our relationship with God. When we fail to take Him at His Word, our lack of trust also is disrespectful, and the opposite of worship. This is sin rooted in immature faith. Let us choose to believe that we can trust God. Let us choose to have Him direct our thoughts.

"Finally, brothers, whatever is true, whatever is honorable, whatever is just, whatever is pure, whatever is lovely, whatever is commendable, if there is any excellence, if there is anything worthy of praise, think about these things." (Philippians 4:8)

"Love is patient and kind; love does not envy or boast; it is not arrogant or rude. It does not insist on its own way; it is not irritable or resentful; it does not rejoice at wrongdoing, but rejoices with the truth. Love bears all things, believes all things, hopes all things, endures all things." (1 Corinthians 13:4–7)

We're all trying to be more like Jesus—full of strength and dignity, and yet laying down our lives for others in service. It is a mystery. But no, respecting your husband does not make you a doormat. It makes you obedient.

How About You?

1. *Review the proverbs about fools and reflect for a moment. What events or conversations from your*

life has the Lord brought to mind? How would practicing the discipline of silence have potentially improved the outcome of your situations?

2. *What have you learned about your relationship with yourself during the practice of silence? Are you your own encourager? Or are you useful to the enemy by discouraging yourself? Are your conversations with yourself mostly positive or negative?*

3. *Recall a time when you failed to take your husband at his word and assumed more than he meant. What emotional triggers were embedded in your thoughts or responses to him?*

4. *If you verbalized your thoughts, how did he respond? If you internalized the misunderstanding, how did you process through your thoughts in silence with God?*

5. *As you read through the previous dares, did any of them present an extra challenge? Explain.*

6. *Write your prayer requests in your journal.*

Chapter Dares:

Dare 1: Continue to include the practices of silence, apology, and forgiveness in your communication with your husband. These should be done daily.

Dare 2: Begin changing your habits of thinking by keeping a running list with you at all times. Write down

things you are grateful for as God reveals them to you. Ask God to help you count your blessings throughout each day. Focus your mind on whatever is true, honorable, just, pure, lovely, commendable, excellent, and anything worthy of praise. Teach your children to do this as well, by pointing out the beauty in God's creation. In creating this habit, you will find yourself more joyful and perseverant. Ann Voskamp has an amazing book on this topic.[43]

---

[43] *1000 Gifts* by Ann Voskamp

Truth #12:

Wise Women Do Hard Things To Create Healthy Relationships

Raising teenage boys has provided me with countless opportunities to embrace respectful behavior. Failure to do so quickly creates distance in our relationships, and I'm still learning. I remember when one of my sons was struggling with a friend of his. I listened to his complaints, his emotions, and his angst over the situation. Standing far outside the forest, I had a perspective he did not have. I deeply wanted to help him; however, I knew that I needed to be invited into that opportunity.

One of the first adult behaviors teenagers seem to pick up is feeling disrespected when offered unsolicited advice. This feels like being treated like a child and makes them pull away from us. In other words, I realized I had two choices—I could "mother" him and tell him what I knew, or I could gently knock at a back door and ask for permission to enter, as I would with another respected adult. I chose the latter. It made all the difference in the world.

I empathized with his feelings, reiterating them back to him. He clarified a few things and I responded. I told him I would be praying for him. After giving him some time and the space of a day, I went back to him. "I've been thinking and praying about your situation with your friend. I had an idea, don't know if it is a good one, but if you are interested, I can share it with you." He wanted to hear it and invited me into his world.

He could have said, "Okay. Thanks, I'll let you know," in which case I would have backed off. In practicing this consistently, sometimes he comes to me now and asks me for advice. I feel privileged to have that kind of influence in his life. Like our relationship with God, I need to be open to the leading of the Holy Spirit. I love it that my kids are open to my leading.

Honestly, it is easier to see this opportunity with our teenagers than with the people we married. Sometime during puberty, they start resisting being told what to do. Their souls cry out for respect. If we respond well to these challenges and treat them with greater respect, we earn even more of their trust and build our relationship for the next stage.

I failed to realize, however, that over time, I stopped doing these simple respectful things in my marriage. I stopped asking Jim's opinion about things that affected him. I stopped doing fun friend things with him. I left him a list of chores to do while I was out, as if he were a child. I gave him unsolicited advice and didn't empathize with him when he confided in me about work struggles. I became more critical. We thought we were doing well because the drift was slow.

While I had been practicing active respect in a few ways, I had started taking my relationship with my husband for granted. I stopped asking permission to enter his world. He also had done these things with me and both of us were contributing to an unhealthy atmosphere in our relationship. Revelation 2 specifically tells us that one of the issues Christ has with His church is that we have stopped doing the things we did at first. I firmly believe one can transfer that application to the marriage relationship.

"I know you are enduring patiently and bearing up for my name's sake, and you have not grown weary. But I have this against you, that you have abandoned the love you had at first. Remember therefore from where you have fallen; repent, and do the works you did at first. If not, I will come to you and remove your lampstand from its place, unless you repent." (Revelation 2:3–5 ESV)

Working to fix the issues in your marriage is important – and the sooner you make a decision to be proactive and deal with them, the easier it will be to fix. Understand that you have made a covenant with God, and so you need to figure out how to fulfill the long-term commitment.

Understand that self-centered behavior is the enemy, not your husband. *Marriage is a conflict with your own selfish nature, a context through which God will mature you both. Choose to embrace this opportunity and you'll grow.*

We also have to remember that marriage is a marathon, not a sprint. We will have periods of time where things are difficult and one of the two will carry the relationship because of the other being distracted. Men often experience this when their wife has the first baby. Women see this when their husband focuses on his career. People get sick, careers have issues, children take time and focus, and we both need to be committed to a long haul of maintenance toward our covenant with God. My heart breaks when I hear stories of men or women who leave their marriages because of selfish reasons like their spouse lost his job, his wife got cancer and became needy, or a child dies and the couple blames each other instead of clinging to each other. There are seasons of healing and growth that can go on for a few years. Be tough.

Think about it like this – if we want to give financially to help others, to love our neighbors, we have to have a strong source of income that enables us to do this. If we want to love others, our kids or our husbands well, we have to have a strong source of love coming into ourselves – and the only source that can accomplish that for the long haul is relationship with God. The relationship with God where we're reading off a laundry list of wants and growing in knowledge of the Bible is good, but missing in that we are not receiving His love for us by learning to listen to Him. Being thankful and being obedient to what we read and actively, daily receiving His love is what will keep our own marriage and family relationships strong. This is why we spend so much time talking about these things in this book and doing them in the Daughters of Sarah® classes!

Perception, Prescription, and Permission

After we spend a significant amount of time with another person, we become comfortable in the relationship. There are many benefits to this level of comfort, but there are also downsides to it. Comfort and familiarity can lead to taking the relationship for granted and result in a drifting away from loving and respectful behavior.

Our perceptions of events are skewed by our life experiences and we can start believing our perceptions instead of checking their validity as we did early in our relationship. We start making assumptions about what the other person is thinking or feeling, prescribing thoughts and feelings as if we are inside his head. We think we know him well enough to label how he feels. We make critical comments or are directive in our communication without asking permission to enter his world.

We fail to realize that our perceptions are often wrong; our prescriptions are frequently inaccurate; and we should never stop asking permission before giving advice, no matter how familiar we are with another person!

Early in our relationship, Jim and I spent many hours discussing the minutia of the moments. I remember being very careful in how I presented an opposing position and neither of us assumed we knew how the other felt. We asked questions and listened well. I was careful to not come across as disrespectful and he behaved lovingly.

Somewhere along the line, maybe a year into the marriage, our pride set in. We had become prescriptive in how we communicated our perceptions of each other's behaviors. "You are mad" or "You disagree totally" or other statements about how the other was feeling entered our conversations. Like unsolicited advice, few people enjoy being told how they feel, especially when the other person is incorrect. Missing from our communication was the gentle perception checking we did in the past: "I might be wrong about this, but it seems as if you are feeling angry with what I just said" or "I might be misreading you totally, but is something I said making you nervous?"

I was committing the sin of pride. I thought I knew my husband so well that I knew how he felt and what he thought. I was wrong. Even if I had labeled his emotions or thoughts correctly, it is not respectful to be prescriptive when communicating with other people.

I also was missing an opportunity to see deeper truth by not paying attention to my own feelings. I was issuing blame and criticism, instead of recognizing that I was having a negative response, and, most importantly, that I could be wrong in my perception. "I might be wrong here, but what you said is making me feel really defensive. I heard that I am xyz. Is that what you meant to communicate?"

My husband is a logistics guru for a major US corporation. He has traveled around the world providing expertise and problem solving to various departments of his company. When he hears anything, no matter how positive, his mind naturally and immediately goes to the logistics involved. When I was asked to speak at a regional convention for our denomination and shared this with him, he had twenty questions, none of which I had answers to. The conversation derailed quickly with both of us feeling awful about the interaction. A few months after that interaction, I had learned about the prescriptive nature of our perspectives. An opportunity to be interviewed by a large media outlet arose.

Again, his logistics mind kicked into gear, but this time, armed with new information, things went differently. When we launched into the logistics of the event, I was able to communicate differently. I realized I was taking his questions negatively. "I feel like I've done something wrong, when this is something we could be celebrating." He apologized, congratulated me, and reassured me that he was thrilled about it and very supportive. He affirmed this later by repeating his apology later that night. I realized his questions were important to the process and keeping our family functioning while I was away. I was able to attribute value to his questions and to him, instead of choosing to feel attacked.

Before we recognized the drift in our marriage and got help, we would find ourselves "stuck" in these conflict situations, failing to adequately resolve them. The lack of resolution left us both in a place where we needed to work through things, but could not because very early in the discussions, things were going awry and neither of us knew what to do. Wise enough to get some outside help, we sought assistance from a counselor. The counselor pointed out our habits of prescription and negative perception, while reminding us both about the respectful behavior of asking permission. We were both blind to these behaviors—and recognizing them made all the difference in the world.

We chose to claim a new habit of respectfully asking for permission before giving feedback. This is the only way to offer constructive helps to another person (also known as advice). Instead of critical statements about each other's behaviors, we started discussions by asking permission. "Can I talk about something you did that is bothering me?" or "Do you want some help with that?" and then respecting the other person's response.

Jim approached me one time and said, "Do you mind if I bring up something that is bugging me about how you are acting?" I said, "Sure," and was ready to listen. He said, "I set up a system for the kids to clean the kitchen and dining room after dinner, and I might be wrong here, but I don't feel like you support me in this. You make comments about how everyone should do it differently, and I feel like you are undermining my effort."

I had no idea I was even doing it; although, I was aware I wasn't happy with the mess left in the kitchen. After I thought about my behavior for a moment, I discovered he was right! I had been whining about the quality of the work being done and the system, while the kids were in the process of carrying out their various tasks. I responded to him first, then to the situation. "I am so sorry! You are right, I'm not being supportive of what you did and I'm sure I would feel undermined too. You set up the system, communicated it to them, and I am whining about it before they even get started. You are right. I'm really sorry. I'll stop doing that."

And while I was apologizing and empathizing, I also wondered why I was not happy. What was the problem? And then I knew. So I took action. "Honey, you know, the issue is that while you did set up the system, they aren't doing everything completely. I'm coming into the kitchen to get a drink of water before bed and finding the job unfinished. As a result, I'm cleaning the kitchen at ten o'clock at night. Can you follow up with them and manage their completion of the cleanup so they do a good job?"

He agreed. It was super easy and no one was offended. He did a number of things right, including asking permission to speak into my world. He then talked about his perception and how he felt without accusing me of anything.

Influence

In the situation regarding the kitchen cleanup, I did something right, too, something really important to relationships—I allowed him to influence me. Instead of choosing a posture of defense and having to be right, I chose to allow him to be a treasured child of God who also could be right about something. I chose to allow his perspective to influence my behavior.

I have relationships with a number of women who are gifted in various ways. When I need organizational help, I call Gail. When I need first aid help, I call Sally. When I need parenting help, I call Debbie. When I need physical help, I call Hillary. When I need carpool help, I call Angie. When I need prayer, I call Bonnie. When I need ministry help, I call Beth. The list goes on and on.

Why are we so afraid to allow our husbands to influence us? I think our culture does such a fine job of teaching us that men are fools that we are subconsciously afraid to tap into this incredible opportunity to enrich our marriages. Most men like to fix things and to solve problems. Think what it could do for your relationship if you started including your husband in your list of resources when you need advice! If you want to quickly and positively improve your husband's perception of how you view him, start asking him for advice. As he cares for your family as much as you do, shouldn't he have a say in some of the decisions you make?

I know this is not the context in which this scripture is commonly used, but God used 1 Corinthians 14:35 (KBV): *"And if they would learn anything, let them ask their own husbands at home,"* to encourage me to ask my husband for advice, especially involving our family or our ministry. We often ask each other for advice and achieve what we call "God's best" as a result of including each other in the decision-making process and being open to being influenced by each other. This assists with our parenting as we can be a unified team when dealing with the kids.

When my husband made a pot of chili for dinner one weekend, he accidently left it on the stove on high as he ran outside to do something for thirty minutes. The chili burned a little bit, and, at one point he asked me, "If I do something like this again, leaving something on the stove, is it reasonable to expect you to stir it? Will you just do that for me all the time without me having to ask?" I looked at him and said, "I would like to be able to do that for you, but I can't guarantee I'll remember. But if you ask me each time, I will be happy to do this for you. I sometimes have no idea when you are cooking, or when you go outside, and so if you want me to take care of something for you, you need to ask."

He agreed that made sense. While I could have chosen to be influenced by him, the request did not make sense in the way he presented it. Instead, we ended up with a solution that worked for both of us. Neither of us enjoy losing our memories as we get older, but it certainly endears us to each other's limitations!

I noticed that the basic communication skills I taught in corporate America often fall by the wayside in marriage. I taught leaders how to gently influence others' behavior, how to help the people they managed feel good about the work they were doing. I naturally did this with my teenagers, but had become lazy in my relationship with my husband. We have a unique position of influence in our relationships with the men we married. God has asked us to be our husbands' "helper-completers" but we do a lousy job of this by bossing them around, mothering them, or otherwise trying to shove our opinions down their throats. Then we try the opposite extreme, that of "simply serving" or "martyrdom," telling ourselves, *He doesn't want my help anyway, so I'll just be his slave.*

Both of these extremes are lies and rooted in a lack of understanding of relationship with God and acceptance of His love for us through the gift of Christ. God wants us to speak into the lives of each other and we have a better chance of doing this when we speak respectfully. Just because I have the right answer to a problem my husband has been struggling with does not mean he wants to hear it! I need to ask permission to enter his world, and, when I do, I need to gently present the idea. In this way, we are equipped to live out Proverbs 27:17 (NIV): *"As iron sharpens iron, so one person sharpens another."*

Jim then sometimes seeks out my opinion because we have clearly communicated I am not trying to compete with him in any way, and I can be trusted. A simple, "I've been thinking about this [problem] and praying about it for a while. I might have an idea for you, although it is probably something you already thought about, but if you'd like to hear it . . ." or "I was wondering about that [issue]. I don't know if this would work in your situation, but something I remembered (credible source) suggested was..."

Obviously it's not important who gets credit for the idea.

Repair Attempts

Our counselor also witnessed our inability to make "repair attempts" when a discussion held a lot of emotion and conflict.

"Repair attempts" are the small verbal movements we make toward each other and stopping the conflict in the midst of it. They are the little acts of grace, attempts to diffuse frustration, allowances for the other to save face in an interaction. This is significant, because according to research by Gottman,[44] failure to do this often results in greater pain for both people.

These are high-level communication skills that assume you have mastered the ability not to say mean and sarcastic

---

[44] Gottman, John, PhD., *"Why Marriages Succeed or Fail"* page 22. This book contains extensive information about repair attempts.

comments to injure your husband on purpose. If you have not mastered the basics of mature polite behavior, at the very least, you should apologize immediately if you do say something damaging. A statement that allows your husband to say how you have hurt him is an effective repair attempt. As mentioned in the video for Daughters of Sarah, this is a brief list of repair attempts that I employed before I was aware of Dr. Gottman's research. I encourage you to read more about this topic in his books and to become familiar with these phrases as they can greatly impact your marriage. The awesome thing about them is that we all have a natural way of making a repair attempt. Here are some of the ones I've used or seen used frequently:

- I might be wrong here, but it is my perception that I just said something that upset you, is that true?
- Can you tell me more?" then listen, empathize, and apologize.
- Stop.
- Oh? Why do you say that?
- You seem something – did I upset you?
- I'm starting to get upset. I need to take a break so I can cool down. Can we pray separately for about 10 minutes and then come back to it.
- I feel like you just said that I'm...is that true?
- I am starting to be afraid of you right now.
- It feels like you are accusing me of...is that true?
- This topic seems to be upsetting. Is that true? Can you tell me more about that?
- That didn't come out the way I wanted it to. I didn't mean what I said. Can I try again?
- Wait. What I said isn't what I mean. Can I say it differently?

- I'm sorry – I'm not going to say this right, and I don't want to upset you, but can you just give me some grace and hear my heart over the top of my words?
- I have to tell you something that might hurt you, and I don't want to, but I feel like I'm supposed to. Know that I love love love you first, and that I don't mean to hurt you, okay?
- I'm going to say this wrong, but I don't know how else to say it. Can you please give me some grace here?
- I want to work through this but I don't know how. I'm just making it worse even though I don't mean to.
- I'm so sorry – I can tell I'm just making this worse. Can I try again?

If his face and his words do not match up—men will often lie about this one—then take a risk and say, "It's my perception that I might have just said something that hurt your feelings. I'm sorry. Can you tell me how what I said affected you?" And then allow him to have his say, without justifying what you said or how you said it. Apologize for hurting him and then move on.

Be on the lookout for your husband's attempts to repair a discussion and allow him to influence you. Often Jim will make a small joke in the middle of a conflict and I have the choice to laugh at myself or stay angry. If I take a break and laugh with him, we are able to move on in a healthier way.

All it took was our counselor friend to point out this opportunity and coach us a bit, and we suddenly had a new awareness of not only our own behaviors, but of each other's as well. These small interventions are necessary to helping a relationship be healthy.

Small Talk

Also missing from our repertoire of communication was the small talk about meaningless little things where we simply agreed with each other. We had stopped being *for* each other. Vanished from our communication were the tiny little conversations about the insignificant and trivial things upon which we could easily agree. I began creating small conversations around the things my husband would say or I knew he was interested in and generated opportunities to simply communicate agreement with him.

"It's supposed to rain this afternoon," he said.

"Oh, I didn't know that," I replied.

"I just washed the car," he complained.

"Oh! I hate how the water beads up and leaves rings," I replied.

"I could have waited until this weekend," he said.

"Agreed," I said.

Even if there were things he said that I really did not agree with, I did not challenge most of them. Being disagreeable over minutia actually damages our relationships.

I also prayed and asked God for a newfound interest in my husband as a person. Prayer grows our basis for being friends, which we are called to be, as mentioned in Titus 2: 3-5 (KBV): *"that aged women likewise be reverent in demeanor, not slanderers nor enslaved to much wine, teachers of that which is good; that they may train the young women to love their husbands, to love their children, sober-minded, chaste, workers at home, kind, being in subjection to their own husbands, that the word of God be not blasphemed."*

I began to show interest in the things my husband was interested in and he began to do likewise. I helped him have interest by occasionally sending him e-mails about something I had shared earlier with him. We started becoming more deeply interested in each other and we rediscovered things we had forgotten and learned new things about each other.

This interest evolved into us becoming each other's most important advisor. Whenever we faced a difficult situation or had a great success, the first person we wanted to share those things with was each other. The longing for intimacy is met in the sharing of joys and suffering, bearing each other's burdens, and celebrating each other's successes.

When we communicate about our perceptions and ask for change by asking permission first, we can impact our relationships in more healthy ways.

How About You?

1. *How prescriptive are you when talking to your husband about his behavior? Do you tell him how he feels or what he was thinking?*

2. *Is he prescriptive towards you? How do you deal with that?*

3. *Do you think you know your husband so well you fully understand his thoughts and feelings? Why would you still want to ask him?*

4. *Do you find yourself blaming others for how you feel? Or do you own and talk about how you feel?*

5. *How could choosing to own your perceptions and talk about your feelings help you in conflict?*

6. *How do you feel when you receive unsolicited advice?*

7. *How often are you on the giving end of unsolicited advice? Do you have an opinion on everything and a need to share it? How does this affect your relationships? If you have overcome this or not struggled with it, explain why:*

8. *What do you sense God wanting you to do in this area? How would that glorify Him?*

9. *How do you receive your husband's influence? Do you discount much of what he suggests? Why do you think that is?*

10. *How have you shut down your husband's input into family matters in the past?*

11. *What would happen if you started treating your husband with more respect in this area by considering his opinions and thoughts before making decisions for the family? If you are good at this already, what is the main benefit?*

12. *What does God want to change for you in this area? What challenges will you face? How will you overcome them?*

13. *When is the last time you were honestly interested in your husband as a person? Most of the communication that takes place is because there is a problem. What can you do to be a better friend to your husband?*

Chapter Dare:

1. Pray for God to reveal opportunities to have a new awareness about these topics. Pray for Him to transform you through this awareness.
2. Ask God to help you communicate during conflict. Try using the phrase, "I might be wrong here, but it is my perception that . . ."
3. *Stop* telling your husband how he feels. Instead of saying, "You are angry," say, "I might be wrong here, but, it is my perception that you are angry. Is that right?"
4. *Stop* giving unsolicited advice. Instead, ask permission to speak into someone's behavior if it is affecting you. *Choose carefully* which things you are going to bring up, and be gentle in your approach, allowing the other person to save face. "Would it be okay if we talked about something that I'm really struggling with? [If he says yes, proceed.] I might be completely mistaken here, but I feel xyz when I [hear you say xyz] or [watch you xyz]."
5. Allow your husband to influence you in ways that respect him and you. Be open to what God will teach you through him.
6. Choose to be aware of any repair attempts from your husband during conflict and then choose to respond positively.
7. Generate your own repair attempts when in conflict by giving him an opportunity to save face.

8. Create opportunities to agree with your husband by generating small talk, especially when he instigates it.

You should be off to a good start in helping your marriage and your relationship with God deepen. If you are doing this book in conjunction with Daughters of Sarah®, the conflict sessions and practice in class will help you take things to an even deeper level. There, you will learn how to speak up, respectfully, when you feel your husband is sinning against you or your children. You will learn appropriate ways to engage in conflict and even how and when to start conflict in order to be of better help and good to your family and your husband. We pray you will persevere. If you have a gap of time between now and when the second part of this process begins, I personally invite you to join me in near daily discussion on these topics on my blog at www.NinaRoesner.com, or our Facebook® page for *The Respect Dare* book series.

I also want to offer a very special invitation to you if you feel called to be a Titus 2 leader of women. We'd love to have you experience training from us and help you step up and encourage other women to do what is right and obedient to God in their homes and within their relationships. Our Titus 2 Boot Camp happens once a year. Check out our website, www.GreaterImpact.org for more details. It is like nothing else you've ever experienced! You'll deepen your relationship with God, learn valuable skills for conflict resolution, and take things up a notch as a group leader. You'll likely meet women who will become your friends for life.

Love to you,

~Nina

About The Author

Nina has seen God's hand at work in the courses He's inspired her to write. Over 95 percent of her participants report improving their relationships with God and others, and becoming more confident. She firmly believes that to be fully productive and have peace, one must live life for the Audience of One, being fully engaged in all the roles He has placed us in. She has found her calling in leaving secular business to write and deliver courses and retreats for Christians at a fraction of the cost of what the same high caliber of training goes for in the marketplace.

Nina has over 20 years in the communications and training industry including 15 years with the largest and most successful training company in the world. She has coached numerous executives and pastors around the country and currently provides leadership for Greater Impact Ministries, Inc. as Executive Director.

Nina's expertise in the classroom as a facilitator, trainer, and coach display her God-given talents. The ministry has recently taken steps to provide *Daughters of Sarah®* to churches around the nation, via video, keeping with Nina and her husband Jim's goals of raising their family together. They met in 1985 and married in 1991 after Nina finished her Master's degree at West Virginia University. She and Jim are privileged to be raising their 3 children, Adam, Bram, and Elizabeth, together in Loveland, Ohio. Though her available dates are relatively few, as her family is her primary concern, Nina can be booked for speaking engagements, courses, or retreats through the ministry website at http://www.greaterimpact.org. She blogs regularly at www.NinaRoesner.com.

Daughters of Sarah®

This book was written to be used in the *Daughters of Sarah®* course from Greater Impact Ministries, Inc. Should you wish to continue pursuing the application of Biblical respect and learning even more about being a wife of strength and dignity, consider bringing *Daughters of Sarah®* to your church either in the Live! format over a weekend, or with the video series.

Topics include:
- wrapping our identity up in the Audience of One's opinion of us, rather than people's opinions
- having a healthy sense of self
- learning to communicate with ourselves, our God and others in healthier ways
- becoming a better listener
- learning to speak the language of respect to ourselves, our God and others
- becoming more of a positive influence in our circle
- deepening our relationships, especially with God and our family
- learning how to deal with conflict within marriage more effectively
- And many more...see www.GreaterImpact.org for more information!

THERE IS MORE.

Have you ever wondered, 'Isn't there more?' There is.

We can help you find it. That's what we're all about. You're not meant to do this on your own.
God created us to rely on Him, but we don't. We fight it. We think we can do it by ourselves
and that maybe God will be proud of us when we figure it out.
Here's the truth: He wants to do it with us. Through us. He has a plan for each of us.
Join us and receive training, teaching and knowledge that will change how you live your life. We
listen and offer feedback, and celebrate with you as God does truly big stuff. With Him, you can
make a greater impact. In your marriage. With your children. At your workplace.

FOR WIVES.   FOR SMALL GROUPS.

GreaterImpact™

Redefining Training To Redefine Lives

554 Belle Meade Farm Drive · Loveland, Ohio 45140 · 513.310.6019 · www.greaterimpact.org

facebook.com/RespectDare   @NinaRoesner   pinterest.com/NinaRoesner
                                #daughtersofsarah

Small Group Leader's Guide

This book is written such that the questions are ones that can easily be used in small groups without a great deal of preparation on your part, as long as you are comfortable with the content and women's struggles. We suggest purchasing the *Daughters of Sarah®* Video series which will give you exercises and activities to enhance your group's experience. Do one to two chapters a week if doing this in a group without the videos and other materials. When facilitating a small group, keep these things in mind:

1. Stress confidentiality to all your group members every single week. Make it the first thing you do when you get together. You might say something like, "We want to have an environment where we can be transparent and share, so our one rule is that whatever is shared here, stays here. You are encouraged to talk about what we're doing, but do it in a way that doesn't identify any specific individual." Reminding them of the confidentiality in this way allows them to talk things over with their spouse, a sister, or other friend, but also protects the identity of the group members.

2. You should open each session with a short prayer, inviting God to be present and lead your discussion. You also should feel the freedom to pray for individuals as the session is going on if someone is extremely upset about a situation, etc.

3. Do not offer advice, but rather turn the women in your group back to God's advice. If someone is asking what she should do about something, then encourage discussion about what the Bible says, rather than allowing the women to offer a bunch of opinions. Have a concordance handy or a topical index so you can look things up rather quickly if need be.

4. Don't put anyone on the spot when asking the questions. You might even consider beginning by asking something non-threatening like, "What did you think of the dares for this week?"

5. Don't go around the table or room for input. Instead, allow women to contribute as they feel led. Be careful not to put someone on the spot.

6. Ask open ended questions, rather than questions that end with, "Yes," or "No."

7. At the end of your meeting time, ask for prayer requests for the women to pray over between meetings. It is okay to go around the room at this time.

8. Be transparent as a leader, but be careful not to monopolize the time talking about yourself. It takes at least six seconds for the human brain to respond to a question, so wait a bit before jumping in with your own examples or responses. If you start answering first early on in the meetings, your group will expect you to do this each week and then will not share as easily.

9. Be in prayer about each of the women in between meetings, and have a friend or two pray for you specifically while you are leading your group.

10. Do what you can to attend a Daughters of Sarah® Boot Camp. You'll grow in your ability to lead small groups and help women grow closer to God and improve their relationships.

If you have questions, please feel free to email us at Information@greaterimpact.org .

Be sure to join our community by subscribing to Nina's blog at www.NinaRoesner.com!

74968342R00117

Made in the USA
Columbia, SC
14 September 2019